Travel Bites

Rex Mangin

Books by Rex Mangin

Available as paperback and e-book

Infidelity Gun Running & Other Tales

Cold War Warrior

Flying The Pacific

Mercenary

Albert McConachie's Bad Day

Carrie Gray

Travel Bites

Contents

Foreword

Travel; do it while you're young, and do as much as you can. Better still get into an occupation that involves travel, lots of travel, all over the world. Don't put it off until the blue rinse zimmer frame years.

I'm four score years and then some. I'm a happy chappie, I've travelled; a lot! and it all happened when I was on the right side of sixty.

Europe in my youth. I was a pilot in the military, it took me all over the world before my twenty-fifth birthday. Then a long period with an airline, all over the world again, including periods of living abroad, then early retirement and a lot of cruising. I've done it all, I'm content, don't have that unfulfilled 'bucket list' that seems to be the bane of a lot of my friends.

I did not plan my life like this, it just happened, and I'm glad it happened. Could have stayed at home, got into something that made me a lot of money, worked my guts out, and when I was financially secure, thought about travelling. The trouble with that scenario is that by the time you are financially secure you're getting on in years and the ability to enjoy yourself, really enjoy yourself, can be somewhat restricted.

There is a downside to my scenario however, money. My stay at home friends are mostly well placed financially and are now contemplating spending it. I've already spent it, but I did it at an age where I could really enjoy the experience. These days I don't need much; just as well because there isn't much. The travel bug has been well and truly satisfied and at four score plus years, a bit of the fun has gone out of the traveling thing. That's not completely true.

I would like to go back to Istanbul, and I have a bit of a hankering to go marlin fishing off the Northland coast again, did a lot of it when I had my own boat.

Right now I'm sitting at home looking out at a bleak winter's day, heavy passing showers and freezing cold. Nice and warm inside though, centrally heated. I'm editing my latest book and reflecting on my good fortune in life, I'm content. My friends are going on about their next overseas trips, ticking off their bucket lists. None of it gets me excited, I've done it all. It's a nice feeling.

Writing, I've taken up writing, love it. and I've got a mother lode of memories to call upon. Draft2Digital, they're amazing, produce lovely paperbacks for peanuts.

Delphi

We drove west out of Athens, four of us, two couples. Delphi's the destination. I did not know anything about the place, had not done my homework, however, one of our group had. She filled us in on the detail of what we were about to experience. One of the marvels of the ancient world, probably the most significant archaeological site from that time.

It was hot as we drove through the parched and barren countryside, nothing green in sight, vastly different to New Zealand. We seemed to be out in the middle of nowhere, winding through valleys and up steep hills on the north side of the Gulf or Corinth, then suddenly, a village, perched precariously on a hillside, way up at two thousand feet, Delphi. Looked ordinary, just another small

Athenian Treasury

Greek village in the hills. It did have a 'touristy' look about it, then, just beyond the village, wow! On the side of the steep hill was this huge archaeological site, Delphi. Pytho, the ancient Greeks called it. They considered it the centre of the world. There is evidence of human habitation going back three thousand years. Some of the structures go back to the eight century BC. The place has been invaded and sacked many times over the millenniums. There are the remains of hundreds of impressive stone structures. Further up the steep slope of Mount Parnassus, there's a stadium, the Stadium of Delphi, it could seat six and a half thousand people. It's where the Pythian Games were staged between the sixth and fourth centuries BC. We wandered around awed by what must have been. There was a huge amphitheatre that could seat thousands, spas, and

The Temple of Apollo

the Athenian Treasury, built of Parian marble, where the ancients stored the spoils of war.

5 Delphi

The ancient Greeks were pagans and revered the god Apollo, son of Zeus, God of the sky. Pytho, or Delphi, was originally founded as a place where Apollo could be worshipped and a temple was erected in the fifth century BC. There have been several temples built on the original site. Over the millenniums fires and earthquakes destroyed them, there have been several rebuilds.

Delphi's setting, high on a hillside, is spectacular. Looking out across the deep valley imparts a sense of vastness, of grandeur, something that must have impressed the ancients; a worthy place for the gods.

It was hot and our wandering around amongst the ruins, imagination running free, made us more than a little thirsty so we left the archaeological site and walked along to the present-day village for a beer and something to eat. There we ran into some Australians. They were from a cruise boat anchored down the mountainside in the Gulf of Corinth, a popular place for cruise ships; a guided tour of Delphi. Their cruise had taken them to Olympia further down the west coast and they told us how the ancient ruins there were remarkably similar to what was here at Delphi. We resolved to take in Olympia before we left Greece. So much to see, so much history in this part of the world, ancient history, far removed from anything in New Zealand.

The Holiday

Bang, zing, the heavy nylon line is wrenched out of the quick release and the outrigger pole springs back, thrashing about wildly, the line falls slack then starts ripping off the big Penn reel.

'Strike.'

'Get the gear in.'

There's a wild scramble to grab the other rods, it's a hook up, a powerful one, there could be a big tangle if we don't get the lines in. We're a kilometre off Avarua in Rarotonga, you don't have to go far in this part of the world to find deep water, and big fish.

'What is it?' 'Don't know, need to get a look at it.'

'Probably a mahi mahi, a big one.'

Line continues to rip off the reel.

The boys are doing some serious unwinding, fishing; the girls? shopping of course, it's market day. We have this charter boat 'till midday and it's only nine in the morning. Four yellowfin in the bin already, all around ten kilos, now we have something big. It's still taking line. There's a thousand meters on the reel, half of it is gone already, time to slow things down. Still don't know what it is. Probably a mahi mahi, the skipper reckons it is, he'll know, he does this every day, his life is complete. Russ is in the chair, lucky devil, he was 'on strike' at the right time, can he cope? We're all watching, critical audience.

We had flown up from Auckland, winter escape, a few days in Raro, then that jewel of the South Seas, Aitutaki. We'd done a deal with a luxury hotel there. It's day two of our Cook Islands holiday.

'Ok Russ, tighten up and slow it down.'

7 The Holiday

It's the skipper, a grizzled Kiwi who's lived in Raro since forever, he must have done this a zillion times, lucky fellow. It's his boat, a forty-foot double ended Canadian design, well suited to the job. We got onto it a couple of days earlier; recommended by a mate in Auckland.

'That's the one if you want to catch real fish.' He was right, there were real fish in the bin already.

Russ pushes the clutch lever up to preset and the rod bends right over.

'Hang on, this thing's pretty lively, can you handle it?'

'What, think I'm a girl?'

'Possibly.'

'You'll keep.'

The fight is on, it's not the easiest landing a big game fish, far removed from snapper fishing at home. Is Russ the man for the job? better be or his life will be hell. He lays into the task, pulling up, winding down.

'Let's see some style Russ.'

'Sure you can cope?'

'Cheeky buggers, just watch, you might learn something.'

A chorus of jeering, 'yeah right, I'm sure we will.' The fight continues, he's doing well but this fish is not easy. There are a couple of runs from the fish and some panting from Russ, he starts to look stressed, mutters something about needing a break.

'Don't be a girl, get it in, we want to see it.'

'You'll see it soon enough.'

Better stop taunting him I think he's feeling the strain, of course he's feeling it, fighting a big fish is seriously hard work.

'Will it help if I stand in front of you and down a cold Steiny?'

'You'll get yours, cheeky bugger.'

'There it is, a mahi mahi, a big one.'

Suddenly we're all serious. The fish had surfaced quite close to the boat, all gold and blue, a beautiful sight. Russ finds a new lease of life and winds carefully, don't want to muck it up now. Actually he's an experienced fisherman, caught big fish before. We're confident he's the man for the job, don't want to lose this one.

'Ok, careful now, it's almost at the back of the boat.'

'Yep, it's big, don't see many like this.'

The decky, a local lad, hangs over the side with a big gaff. Russ winds in some more, there's an explosion of action, a lot of splashing, crash, a big mahi mahi, an enormous mahi mahi, lands in the cockpit. The skipper grabs the tail and twists it up quite savagely towards the head. Tail twisting is quite effective in subduing it then he clubs the fish with a big wooden axe handle. Mahi mahi are dangerous when they're landed, there's a long history of fishermen having chunks bitten out of their legs by mahi mahi.

'Look at that, geezz you're just so good Russ.'

'I know.'

'Got a shovel, the s—t's starting to pile up.'

It was a good fish, as big as they get. Green, gold and blue colouring, beautiful. The dolphin fish, that's what they call them. Very thin, almost skinny, about ten centimetres through, but tall and long, almost as long as Russ, that's the shape they are, not very heavy for their size, excellent eating.

'Well let's down one,' celebration time. God, we're going to have to suffer Russ now.

It's beers all 'round and it's only ten in the morning, not a problem, holiday time, no responsibilities, no 'list of jobs I want you to do dear.' Cameras, pictures, catch that colour before it fades.

'Come on girls, have your picture taken with Russ, and his fish, he's just the greatest, ask him.' The girls are at the wharf, must have sensed our return. It's nostalgia photo time, you know, the old sepia tinted pictures of great uncle Russ and his big fish. The mahi mahi is hauled up on the scales, 17kg, it is a big fish, as long as Russ, lots of photos.

Our good Captain deals to one of the yellowfin. Quartered, skinned, and sliced into very thin sashimi. In no time at all there's a plate of fresh yellowfin sashimi, complete with Wasabi and Soy sauce, right on the wharf, how fresh is that, and how delicious!

'Now that was real fishing!'

'Well girls, how was the shopping?'

'Look at that.' He was spinning around on his shoulders, upside down, rap music blaring, breakdancing Rarotongan style. The dancer could not have been more than eight or nine years old. We were captivated, this little fellow was good. He sprang to his feet, arms and legs going every which way, perfectly in synch with the music, he had rhythm. There's a backup band, mums and dads, but the music at the moment was all electronic rap. We were at the Saturday market, an institution in Avarua. There was this small stage where the locals could strut their stuff, there were plenty of takers. The girls had dragged us along, I was glad they had, it was fascinating.

The fish? We left it with our skipper, that's the deal when you charter a boat. You can take your fish with you, if you want, but really, what would you do with it, there was a lot of fish. The skipper had deals with a couple of restaurants where he makes a little extra on the side. Fish does not command much of a price in Raro, it's so plentiful. The local supermarket sells yellowfin for around five dollars a kilo, *five dollars*, in New Zealand it's forty-five.

Dance show over, the mums and dads start strumming, the atmosphere changes from electronic pop to South Seas, *this is the South Seas*. We wander around the stalls, fruit, paw paw, look at the paw paw, they're huge, and ripe. I love paw paw and these ones are as good as they get. At home they're a disaster, green, tasteless, quite often hard, with lumps inside, they definitely don't come from Rarotonga, pity. *A dollar each! five dollars at home.* There are mangos, pineapples, bananas, all beautifully fresh, and cheap, well compared with Auckland that is. We should buy some, take them back to the hotel, no, not practical, another time perhaps.

'Here we are, a shirt shop.'

'Russ, over here, this place has your shirt.'

'Really, let's have a look.'

Plenty of brightly coloured shirts on display, run by an attractive local, well she looked like a local until she spoke, born and raised in Papatoetoe, up here for a couple of months.

'You lucky thing, you've got it made.'

'I know,' she says.

'Russ here needs this green and gold one with the mahi mahi all over it and I think we need these matching black and white tees.'

'You do good deals for Kiwis?'

'Everything's a good deal here' she replies.

'We know, but we want a real deal, big order, four shirts.'

'Kiwis; my best deal, sixty dollars.'

I pull out a fifty-dollar note and wave it about.

'Going for fifty, once, twice.'
'No, not going; sixty,' she says.
'Fifty, come on we're poor kiwis.'
'Yeah right, ok fifty-five,' she offers.
'Done, you're a good girl.'
We try the shirts on, matching black tees with a white fern motif. Russ gets the colourful green and gold one emblazoned with a mahi mahi leaping out of the water. We leave our new shirts on and bag the 'fishy' ones.

The place could be the Otara car park on a Saturday morning. The stall keepers had Kiwi accents and New Zealand currency was used. It seemed they all lived in Auckland. Imagine dividing your time between Auckland and this place, I could handle that.
'Where are the girls?'
'Probably over at the jewellery stalls.'
'There are some really good black pearls there, I've had a look.'
'That could get expensive.'
'Don't need any more pearls, enough of them at home already.'
We round up the girls and head for Trader Jack's, an institution in Avarua, a 'must visit.' Good place for lunch and it's well into lunchtime.
'Can you seat eight?'
'Sure can, follow me.'
A big round table on the balcony, right over the water, spectacular.
'Some beer perhaps, quench the thirst?'
'Eight Heineys please.'
We peruse the menu, very tempting, all sorts of good things. I'm really hungry, it's been a long time since that scratch breakfast.
'There's mahi mahi Russ, reckon it could be yours? it says *fresh* mahi mahi.'
'Could be, wonder if they do BYO fish.'
'You'll have to have it Russ, matches your flash shirt.'

'Yellowfin, see that, says fresh as well.'

'Girls, try our fish, it'll be good, we only catch the best.'

We order fish and a savvy blanc. I notice yellowfin tatami amongst the entrees, that could be a taste thrill, yellowfin tatami's as good as it gets.

The surf's crashing in right in front of the balcony. There's no outer reef along this part of the coast, no protection from the full force of the sea, something that's caused the restaurant's owner, Jack, problems in the past. The place has been destroyed several times by tropical cyclones, each time Jack has rebuilt it. We sip our beer and enjoy the sun, the boys reminisce about the morning's fishing, the girls talk shopping. The place is full, Trader Jack's is popular, been going for years. The owner, a Kiwi, can usually be found propping up the bar, he's a colourful character.

A couple of years earlier I had enjoyed a few beers and a yarn with Jack, he told me about some of the difficulties of running the restaurant. No insurance company will take it on so Jack had taken matters into his own hands and come up with his own innovative solution. Usually there's plenty of warning of a tropical cyclone. The main components of Trader Jack's can be dismantled and removed in just a few hours. The bar can be lifted right out of the building and the big folding windows across the front are on quick release fittings and easily removed. The some applies to all the main parts of the kitchen and restaurant. When everything's taken out there's just the thick concrete floor left standing on concrete piles, this survives, well so far it has, the outer wooden structure of the building is sacrificial. Replacing it after a storm is part of the cost of doing business in this part of the world. Recently, however, Jack got caught, a rogue wave, a big one, out of the blue, no warning. It crashed right into the restaurant and did a lot of damage. A hard place to do business all right!

13 The Holiday

The wine arrives, ice bucket on a stand, a Giessen from Marlborough. Blenheim's my home town. I should be a substantial landowner in the Wairau valley; if only!

The Tatami I ordered arrives, nice reddish centre, black pepper encrusted edging, thinly sliced and plenty of it.

'Can I try a piece?' from one of the girls.

'There's a price!'

'Anything you say.'

Shrieks of laughter.

'Can we watch?'

'Watch what; the eating or the payment?'

'Now now, this is a nice party, we're eating food here.'

The Tatami was good, very good, eat your hearts out.

The waitress appears with large plates piled high.

'Mahi mahi?'

'Yours Russ, I can see your thumbprint.'

'Tuna?'

'Yep, over here.'

Mahi mahi fillets and yellowfin steaks, how good does it get.

'Excuse me, I think we need another bottle, make that two.'

We continue on. It's nice and warm in the sun, surf crashing on the sand, soft background music, it really is a first-class place for lunch. Some children are racing each other in canoes out in front of the restaurant, and there's some boat movement in the small harbour next door.

'Now listen up, the word is a visit to Whatever's is a bit different.'

'Where's that?'

'Across the creek, up the stairs.'

'Think we should?'

'I've heard it's an experience.'

'What is it?'

'A bar; with a difference.'

'A bar! that settles it, let's go.'

Different alright. On a rooftop, open air, fantastic view, rough and ready. The characters in the place, no ordinary people, everyone's a character. Some beat up trestle tables, a few decrepit chairs, and a covered bar across one end. A couple of hard case locals are talking loudly nearby, weather-beaten faces, long white hair.

'Welcome to Whatever, from Auckland?' it's the barman, perceptive fellow.

'Of course, is there anywhere else?'

'Yep, definitely Auckland, cheeky, probably don't like Winston either.'

We front the bar and order some drinks, the place has character to burn, and atmosphere. The barman, a local, friendly fellow, sharp wit and talkative.

'Take a seat, no don't steal it, just sit on it, wouldn't want to lose any of the period furniture.'

He brings the drinks. We enjoy the sunshine and the remarkable view, very different place to Jack's.

'What happens when it rains?'

'You get wet; where did you go to school?'

We get into conversation with the two locals, they're Rarotongans with Kiwi accents, spend a lot of time in New Zealand, I think everyone in Rarotonga does. One of the weather-beaten chaps reckons he owns an island. Winston is his hero, remember the Wine Box? well it's part of Rarotongan folk law now. His white-haired mate reckons he's talking bullshit, he's chuckling away, I think they'd both been sitting in the sun drinking for quite a while, not sure if it was the beer or the sun. They take a shine to our girls who respond in kind. Suddenly we have a very friendly little gathering on the rooftop, more beer, this on top of all the wine, it's holiday time.

'Nobody leaves without a T shirt,' the barman announces.

'Let's have a look?'

A selection of Ts and singlets, all black with WHATEVER emblazoned across the chest, a 'must have' item if you've been here. We all get into the act, there's a lot of trying on and critical appraisal. Decisions are made, alcohol impaired decisions, hope they are ok? purchases follow, the barman is pleased. That's two shirts I've bought today, I thought we were just going fishing.

'I need a nana nap,' it's Russ.

'What, worn out by a fish?'

'Yep, bit jealous are we?' Russ responds.

'Actually that's a good idea, I think it's the yacht club at Muri for dinner, more drinking. I'm full as a bull already.'

We take our leave from Whatever's.

'We'll be back.'

'Of course you will, you guys obviously appreciate a good bar.'

The Sailing Club at Muri right on the lagoon beach, the loveliest part of Rarotonga, good restaurant as well. Early evening, we are camped on the club's big wooden deck sipping cocktails, well the girls are, the boys, beer. There's still sailing activity out on the lagoon, picture postcard stuff.

'How was the nana nap Russ? sure you were napping?'

'You'll keep.'

Dinner, not really hungry, perhaps a light meal, we're off to Aitutaki in the morning.

Aitutaki, that jewel of the Pacific, a beautiful place. I've been there several times and it is the most beautiful place on earth, the perfect corral atoll set in a magic ocean. Aitutaki lagoon is huge, a ring of motus, small coral islands, that form the outer reef and there's a larger island where the locals live.

Ouch, sore head, will I ever learn. We had lingered on a bit too long at Muri, the light meal turned into a rather substantial affair, and there was wine, too much wine. Our hotel deal has us staying at The Pacific Resort Aitutaki, an upmarket boutique hotel. We had secured it at a very competitive price, this could be good. I've never stayed at a top of the line boutique resort, some very good hotels sure, but not at a place like this. We flew north across the incredibly blue Pacific, forty-five minutes and Aitutaki comes into view, a magic white circle of breaking surf surrounding a huge sparkling lagoon. We land and are greeted by a fellow singing and playing a ukulele, great atmosphere. The hotel people round us up, we're off to paradise. The entrance to the Pacific Resort says it all, luxurious, spectacular, waterfalls, tropical vegetation, a welcoming speech, fruit cocktails, then off to our bures. They're set amongst thick vegetation at the top of the most perfect beach. Each bure opening directly onto its own private piece of beach, two sun lounges, just for us. The bures are upmarket, island décor, impressive wood carvings, pictures, artwork, a modern bathroom, fully stocked mini bar, all the trimmings. A large deck in front discreetly designed for maximum privacy, right on the beach, very comfortably furnished, upholstered lounge chairs, beach towels, fresh water shower by the beach steps, yes indeed this place is top notch. We settle in, check the mini bar, and enjoy a cool drink out on the deck. The view across the lagoon to the distant reef, the crashing surf, the warm sunshine filtering through the overhanging trees, how good does it get?

A swim. Down a couple of steps onto the beach, a wide expanse of perfect white sand, flat water, and a whole lot of small tropical fish, water temperature just right. The Aitutaki experience was getting better all the time. We float around in the shallows for a while then decide to go along to the main bar. Another delightful experience, a big outdoor bar by a swimming pool. The girls are into the cocktails again, colourful affairs with flowers and little umbrellas. The talk turns to a lagoon cruise, we only have three days here so we need to get onto it right away.

Aitutaki lagoon is probably the most beautiful in the world, it's big and very old, a mature corral atoll. Over the millenniums the lagoon has slowly filled with crushed coral sand, very fine and extremely white, the water is shallow and there's a great depth of this white sand beneath it. The whole place has a shimmering white appearance that's very impressive. A trip out on the lagoon is a must, probably the best experience you can have at Aitutaki. A bit of research and the answer is a Kia Orana Cruise with Captain Fantastic, deal done, booked for the following morning. The rest of the day is spent doing very little, that's why you come to a place like this. That evening we book a poolside table for our group out under the stars, cocktails, beers, an excellent meal, mahi mahi, wahoo, tuna, and the setting, well what can I say, the place is perfect.

Captain Fantastic's lagoon cruise. Breakfast in the main dining room. What a setting, high on a rock outcrop with open sides overlooking the lagoon, I cannot imagine a more impressive setting. Down to the boat in the small harbour, and it is small, a gap in the main reef with a narrow channel that leads into a small mooring area that's been blasted out of the coral, six boats is about the limit. The channel can only be used at the top of the tide. Captain Fantastic is a colourful character, an aluminium runabout fitted with ten seats, bimini sun top, and big outboard motor. We climb aboard and the Captain gives us a briefing.

'We're going out onto the lagoon to do some snorkelling in an area known for its abundance of fish, there are some big clams and a Giant Trevally that usually makes an appearance. After the snorkelling we'll do some beachcombing on a couple of small

motus, some swimming, then a beach BBQ. All seated, let's go.'
We race off across the crystal-clear water dodging the numerous nigger heads that are common in Aitutaki's lagoon, first stop, way out in the middle of nowhere.

'Ok, masks, fins, snorkels, over the side, enjoy the viewing,' and the viewing is great.

There are numerous corral outcrops and zillions of fish, every colour and shape imaginable, the water's warm and amazingly clear, we just hang there looking. On the white sand bottom, not far below, are groups of giant clams, really big ones, they've been introduced into the lagoon from Australia's Great Barrier Reef and are adapting well. The locals are nurturing them the idea being to get a local population established. I did not pick up on the reason for this but it's quite a serious project, the clams certainly added interest to the snorkelling. After a while we gather back at the boat and the Giant Trevally turns up right on cue. No mug this fish, he knows there's a feed in it. The thing is huge, about one and a half meters long, a pale sandy colour pretty much the colour of the lagoon bottom, good camouflage. The boat boy feeds him large pieces of fish that are gulped straight down. All this happens right in front of our masks, an extraordinary sight. The Trevally would not go away, really friendly, just kept circling about coming in close if it thought there might be another morsel, eventually it disappears into deeper water. We climb back aboard and motor off to the next idyllic spot.

A big sand bank, Honeymoon Island, over the side, wade ashore. Our boat takes off, disappears, bit of a worry, however, where we are looks like heaven, a Hollywood movie set. A vast expanse of pure white sand, warm underfoot, a burning sun beating down, there's no shelter, watch out for your skin. We wander about, quite an extraordinary experience. At one end there's a clump of vegetation, some coconut palms and a little undergrowth, as we get closer there's a wooden board with the words Aitutaki Kite School and a telephone number, really. The place is deserted, we are miles from anywhere. Under the palm trees a trestle table and some juvenile sea birds sitting on the sand, they show no fear. There are a lot of nesting birds, the place is a breeding colony. Someone has been here. We find a coconut with one end chopped off, it's been colonised by dozens of hermit crabs that are feeding on the coconut flesh, it's been completely hollowed out. Lots of little shells, all converted into little crab houses, all moving about.

After a while our boat reappears, we get back on board and motor a short distance to another motu, a more substantial affair formed from raised corral seabed. It's heavily vegetated and appears to be a breeding colony, there are young birds all over the place just sitting on the sand under the vegetation. We set off walking around this motu flopping into the sea whenever the going gets too hot, it's magnificent. There's a gathering point on the lagoon side where Captain Fantastic has a small building and BBQ area complete with trestle table and sunshield. We enjoy the next hour or so swimming in the crystal-clear lagoon and lying in the sun while an excellent BBQ meal is prepared, yellowfin steaks, tropical fruit, veg, a superb spread. One of the Captain's boys plays a guitar and sings, he's good. Plenty of picture taking and just enjoying the atmosphere, we really are in the idyllic South Seas, *go to Aitutaki!* Eventually it's time to go back. Along to the resort, poolside bar, cocktails, beer, marvellous day.

Next day, lay day, do your own thing, off we go in different directions. A couple of energetic types cycle around the main island, another couple do it on a scooter, some enjoy a serious sleep in and some just laze about on the beach and the hotel's amazing infinity pool. We take our drinks into the pool and line them up on the pool's edge, impressive spot for a drink. Later we drag the sun lounges down to the water in front of our bure and enjoy a bottle of wine while semi submerged in the ocean, what a way to go. Another thing, no children, I don't know what the resort's policy is but it sure is nice not having kids around.

The previous evening we had enjoyed an excellent meal on a small private balcony attached to the main dining room, we decided a repeat was in order, steak was the popular choice, it was good. During the meal the chef made an appearance, a young local fellow, we praised him for his expertise in the kitchen.

Back to Rarotonga. The Aitutaki experience was almost over, damn. A final splash in the lagoon, throw everything into the suitcase, off. The climb out takes us over the southern end of the lagoon, the picturesque motus surrounded by incredibly blue water, the vividly white beaches, the palm trees, the crashing surf; it is the most beautiful place on earth.

Back at Muri and the word is sunset at Shipwrecks, a 'must see.' It's a small beachfront place on the western side of the island. Shipwrecks is certainly well located, a big sandy beach facing due west, owned and operated by a hard case American fellow. This chap insists he is Rarotongan, calling him American was not appreciated. It transpires he was actually born in Hawaii. He had wall to wall whiskers and wore a straw hat, a 'wild man from the South Seas.' We had heard that his dinner was excellent, however, it only happened twice a week, booking was essential, we resolved to return for dinner. The bar was straight out of Hollywood. Cocktails were served in jam jars, very nice jam jars with 'SHIPWRECKS' on the side, but still jam jars, different! The sunset was as advertised, exquisite.

We booked, and returned the following day for dinner. Aroa Beachfront Inn at Arorangi, that's the full name. The late afternoon setting was magnificent, a few drinks then into the wine. Cookie, a hard case local, had several beer basted chickens on his BBQ. We had a yarn with him and got the low-down on just how to cook a chicken on a beer can, he had spare ribs on the go as well. A lot of photo taking. The sunset was perfect, and the meal, seriously good. Chicken, bacon, spare ribs, a wonderful array of island fruits and salads; we just pigged out that evening. Dinner over, the versatile Rarotongan owner, 'don't call me American,' entertained at the piano, followed by a local girl who sang island songs in Cook Island Maori, she was the highlight of the evening. If you ever find yourself in Rarotonga make a point of booking dinner at Shipwrecks.

There's a rugby game on in New Zealand the following evening, serious stuff. An All Black test match and in rugby mad Rarotonga it was going to be shown live on TV. A decision is made that this game has to be watched. A couple of inquiries and we find out the game can be seen on a big screen at the Muri Rugby Club just down the road.

'We're going.'

'Boring,' from the girls, 'we didn't come to Raro to watch boring old rugby.'

Problem, don't want to upset the girls, but an All Black test; has to be watched. Girls are just not rugby fans.

'How about we all have dinner then the boys go off and watch the game,' a desperate attempt to salvage the situation.

'We'll go up the road to that Pizza place around six, I hear it's good, we can enjoy a meal, then the boys can go and do their thing. It's being televised live from New Zealand, kick off is at 9.30 here, come on girls, that's a good compromise.'

Surly looks, the girls are not overjoyed with this suggestion.

'Well, I guess we could, bit selfish though,' the girls take on it. Success, control yourself, don't show too much enthusiasm.

The pizzas are good, particularly the meat lovers, we ply the girls with wine and the atmosphere improves a little.

'I'm a bit tired, bed would be a good idea,' this from one of the girls, things are looking up.

The boys troop off down the road looking for the rugby club, it's not obvious just where it is, eventually we find it, a big hall, bar at one end, big TV at the other, and an interesting gathering of locals. The TV's a projection job, the picture's terrible, covered in white stuff. It transpires that during a recent redecoration solvent had been splashed onto the projector's lens, the fix would be costly so it had been left as it was, dud picture; that's the way it is in Rarotonga. Certainly put an interesting spin on the game. There were parts that were all a bit of a blur when the action was in amongst the white stuff but we got the general run of play. The locals were very enthusiastic, vocal in their support of the All Blacks. One of the new young Blacks, an island lad, scored a couple of tries, this brought a wild response, they do like their rugby in Rarotonga.

The beer was flowing and a few characters were getting 'friendly.'

'You fellas from New Zealand?' A short chap wearing a beanie, full as a bull, he wanted to talk, up close and personnel, but his beer breath! There was a good time girl in a short skirt, I think she realised early in the piece that our group were a lost cause. I reckon watching the locals was more interesting than the rugby. The game ebbed and flowed, the All Blacks prevailed, great jubilation. More beer, it was cheap, a lot cheaper than our upmarket hotel along the beach. We took advantage of this, not a very bright thing to be doing but we're off the hook, no longer had the restraining influence of the girls.

'Right, home, lets walk along the beach.'
Good idea, but there's no moon, pitch black. We are feeling no pain at this stage, off we go stumbling along in the sand.

'Does anyone know where we are?'

'Rarotonga.'

'Yeah, right.'
Our hotel appears, it's the flares, just as well because it sure is dark.

'Don't make so much noise, shush, don't wake the girls.'

'Got your key?'

'No.'

'Where's my key?'

'I don't know, I think the girls must have them.'

'Hang on, I've got mine, I'll go in and climb around the balcony and let you in.'

'Not sure that's a good idea, Trish will knock your block off if you try climbing over the balcony, she knows about these island boys.'

Suddenly a door flies open.

'Oh, you're back, must you make such a racket.'

Doors open, we all disappear inside, great evening.

Back to Auckland in the morning, heavy passing showers, hail rattling the windows, cold; welcome home.

A Day In Istanbul

It's big and it's right there in front of me, just a pane of glass away. There's a big fellow with a gun right there as well. I'm looking at the Topkapi Diamond, the real one, that's what the man said, hard to believe though, must be a copy, surely!

We're in the Topkapi Palace in Istanbul being crushed by a sea of tourists and a lot of screaming kids. In spite of the distractions, I am impressed. The big diamond, it's actually called the Spoonmaker's Diamond, a huge pear-shaped affair surrounded by a host of lesser stones, it's reputed to be the fourth largest diamond in the world. I'm fascinated, hard to believe it's the real thing. Remember that 1964 film, Topkapi, with Peter Ustinov? No? Well in the movie he attempts a spectacular heist in this place.

What are we doing in Istanbul? We've just disembarked from a cruise boat, a very comfortable 'boutique' cruise boat that we've been on for the past ten days sailing from Venice to Istanbul. Stopped off at all the exotic places en route, there were plenty of them. The cruise bit's over, pity, that boat was good. We're now ensconced in the Arena hotel in the old part of Istanbul for a few days before we fly all the way back to New Zealand, not looking forward to that. A long flight half way around the world is a dog, doesn't get any better as you get older either. Coming over we'd stopped off in Dubai and had a look around, that was really good, broke the long journey. Now we're worn out and looking at a direct flight home. Stop thinking about it, enjoy the sights, there's a lot to see, fascinating place. Definitely put Istanbul on your bucket list.

The Arena hotel. Our good tour organiser did her homework, some research on the Internet, came up with the Arena, she got it right.

We're a group of four, holidays are more fun when you're with another couple. The Arena's in the old part of Istanbul on a small side street quite close to the Hippodrome. All the things you want to see are within walking distance. The Grand Bazaar, Spice Market, Blue Mosque, Hagia Sophia, Topkapi Palace, Golden Horn, there's a lot to take in. We've given ourselves four days, we are going to need every minute of it. The girls have a fixation on the Grand Bazaar, shops, they just can't help themselves, it's in the female genome.

'Let's walk up to the Grand Bazaar.'

'Yes dear;' you find yourself saying this a lot as you get older. Not a silly idea, the walk through the streets is an adventure in itself. Amazing sights, the cameras are going flat out, going to be a lot of picture sorting when this is over. I'm going to need some more film, my small handycam uses tapes. I've stuck with it because I know how to operate it, but the film's becoming hard to get, I guess I'll be updating soon. Anyway, we were making fairly slow progress, there's just so much to see and photograph, the girls are clicking away, I hope they produce some good pictures, those little phone cameras do have their limitations. We stop for coffee at a sidewalk café, it turns into a real experience. The locals quickly identify us as Kiwis, very sharp the Turks. A fellow gives us a long dissertation on New Zealand, he's pretty knowledgeable too. We gather he'd been a crewmember on a ship that had been there. Then there's a fellow who tries very hard to sell us something; can't remember what, but I do remember the performance. More picture taking and its only day one. If it's all like this coffee shop then we're in for an interesting time. We extricate ourselves from the characters in the coffee shop and continue on towards the Bazaar. *Ding ding,* 'look out,' there's a train coming down the road. It's an Istanbul tram, they're different, they run along the centre of the street on rails, big long affairs with two or three carriages in tow. A tram, as I recall, was much smaller and there were no carriages, they used to carry me from downtown

Wellington up to Nana's place in Brooklyn, these Istanbul trams are very different creatures.

We get to the Bazaar, The Grand Bazaar Beyazt, a huge high roofed rambling structure, the oldest and largest covered market in the world, and the most visited tourist attraction, dating back to the fifteenth century. Been burnt down several times and suffered from earthquakes over the centuries, but it's always been rebuilt. Twenty-two entry gates each one crowded with humanity, every nationality imaginable.

I cast my mind back many years. My dear old Mum had been to this very Bazaar, did the big OE fairly late in life after Dad passed away. She purchased a gold necklace right here in this very place, a nice one, very Egyptian in appearance, quite valuable. I remember Mum giving me a lecture many years ago about how, if you knew what you were doing, then this Bazaar was the place to buy gold. We were on the usual restricted Kiwi budget, you know, champagne tastes, beer income, look but don't, *can't,* buy. We had done 'High Tea' at the Burj Al Arab in Dubai on the way over, that alone would have paid for a gold necklace! I often debate with myself, do you collect possessions or experiences as you progress through life, experiences win every time. I'll never forget that 'High Tea' at the Burj.

Enough of the philosophizing, let's hit the shops, well the girls can hit the shops, what are the boys going to do? Follow along of course and take pictures, lots of pictures, the subject matter is endless. But before we go into the Bazaar the girls suggest a toilet stop, this could be interesting.

There's a public toilet near the entrance where we were, that's what the sign said, in several languages, and there was a charge to use it. Muslim country! a hole in the floor, no seat, no toilet paper! The boys used the men's one that was separated from the female's toilet by a flimsy wall, we could hear their shrieks of dismay.

Inside at last. The shops are incredible, everything imaginable is for sale, material shops, rug shops, metal ware shops, furniture shops, there's a shop for everything, oh yes, those gold shops, they're fabulous; there are a lot of them. I wonder which one had caught my dear old Mum's attention all those years ago? The girls are in heaven, targeted by every good keen shop owner. The girls are good, give the shop owners a hard time, it's expected, the shop owners would be disappointed if you did not play along. We spend a long-time shopping; the boys get restless. Girls don't seem to understand this and become a little intolerant of our increasing impatience. It was fascinating looking around, the girls shopping, the men following along and getting a bit fed up, many nationalities, all doing the same thing. Let's face it there's a fundamental difference between the male and female when it comes to shopping.

On a brighter note the boys suggest a parting of the ways. We set up a rendezvous for an hour ahead. I need air. The Bazaar's a great place but I think I've had enough, let's get outside.

The surrounding streets are something else, teeming with life and activity, just standing on a corner watching is incredible. The streets are steep. There are fellows with bikes carrying huge loads, skinny little chaps who must be very strong. Occasionally they exceed their limits and there's a crash. Other fellows are running around with trays of food and drink held high. The idea is for shop owners, and others, to order 'morning tea' from one of these fellows. He will race off and get it for them, seemed to be quite a common practise. There are groups of women out socializing, Muslim women, all wearing burkas and having coffee at the numerous coffee shops, great photo op. I was trying to do just that without making it too obvious, did not need to worry, the women didn't mind at all. We wander around the streets taking it all in then it's rendezvous time, back into the Bazaar, find the fountain we'd agreed on, 'ah, where was it again?' The place is a rabbit warren, alleyways going off in all directions, all look the same. Luck is with us, we stumble onto it, the girls are not there. There's a bench around the fountain, we sit down and observe the passing scene. You will never get bored in Istanbul. The girls arrive, surprise, only a couple of small shopping bags.

It's now mid afternoon, it's suggested we walk along to the Spice Market, another of Istanbul's 'must see' places. Out onto the crowded streets again. Quite a steep walk down to the Spice Market, it's not far, more fascinating street scenes. I'm getting to like this place, so different, and the Turks are very friendly. Roadside kebab places are plentiful, large pieces of meat cooked vertically on a rotating spit. The fellow will slice some off, as much as you want. We walk on and there it is, the Spice Market. There's an inside covered part, and an outside, both were home to the biggest collection of exotic spices, cheeses, strange fruits, small fish, and countless other things that I could not recognise. We wander about absorbing the sights and smells, nothing like it in our part of the world. Coffee time, we pick a likely looking place and try our luck. The Turks are very good, they appreciate that their style of coffee is not necessarily what the rest of the world likes and they offer more 'westernised' options. We enjoy the coffee then another wander around the Spice Market, it just did not seem to get boring, the variety, the colours, great experience, another thing for your bucket list.

Back to the hotel, 'let's walk, it's not far,' walking in this place is an experience. One thing became apparent, well the boys noticed it, no bars, you could get a Coca Cola but try for a beer, forget it. This could be a problem. It was just about cocktail hour and it was hot, a cold beer was in order. Not all bad, you could get a beer, but it required considerable effort to find a place. We asked around and were directed to a place up the street where we were assured we could get cold beer. Off we went, a supermarket, yes, they did sell cold beer. Back to the hotel, up to the rooftop bar where a waiter brought us some large jugs of cold beer. We were lucky, it was a little after six, the bar had opened. During the day they do not sell liquor at all, not even to house guests, we're in a Muslim country, that's the way it is. Across the street there's a tall stone column, very old, just standing there on a weed covered patch of ground, how much history was attached to that column. It appeared to be from ancient times and it made us aware of just how old Istanbul is.

Our first day was drawing to a close, it had been incredible, we have several more days in this great city. Into bed, sleep; 'aahh, what's that noise?' Thump, thump, thump. The noise was caused by car tyres on a cobbled street and it sounded very close. Our room in the Arena was just below street level on an outside wall, the head of our bed was right at street level, about three meters from the actual cobbles. It was a one-way affair, uphill, and the tyre noise was loud, this could be a problem. I pulled the curtain aside and opened the window, I could see peoples' feet, right at eye level about a meter away, and just beyond the feet, the car wheels thumping on the cobbles.

'Close the window.'

'But it's hot and there's just the ceiling fan.'

'Never mind, just close it.'

'*Yes dear.*'

We are in luck; it appears Istanbul's drivers go home early, the traffic noise is all but gone by eleven, at last glorious sleep. That's day one, what a day it was, another day tomorrow.

The SS Angelika

It was a dunga, an absolute dunga, but cheap, and very nasty. Phil said, 'that's the one.' It's going to Crete, Heraklion, that's where we want to go. Tied up in a grubby backwater in Piraeus, it should have been sent to the knacker's yard years ago, end of the line, no self-respecting shipping company would even think about it. Well someone did. The SS Angelika made the Tamahine look like the Queen Mary.

The Tamahine, a bad memory from childhood, another dunga, sailed from Picton to Wellington during the night and only when it was rough. My parents were always going to Wellington, and I was always seasick. I hated that boat.

Four of us from New Zealand, Phil, myself, and his two cousins, a couple of country girls on their big OE, only met them a week ago. Phil said they were nice girls, his favourite cousins, 'and keep your hands off.' Yes Phil, they're safe, horsy types, but nice.

We were slumming in Athens, usual problem, no money, learning how to survive in the Med on the smell of an oily. You get to eat a lot of tomato salads awash with olive oil when you are broke in the Med. They grow great tomatoes and it's the cheapest meal. The plan is to get to Crete, Phil's idea, appealed to me as well, another box ticked. I like the Med, the climate for starters, well the summer climate, and it's cheap. You can get by with very little, just as well because we had very little. Living in Germany at the time, a big Royal Air Force Base at Geilenkirchen. We are both pilots in the Royal Air Force, raising the standard, giving the Poms a bit of stick. Phil comes from Canterbury, a tall lean Ed Hilary type, always coming up with bright ideas, Crete's the latest.

'We're going to Crete, couple of cousins over from home, they want to do Greece, need a bit of chaperoning. The Med's nice at this time of the year.'

'Cousins? Let's see, photos Phil.' He produces a photo, a couple of not unattractive girls.

'Hmm, Crete eh! Sounds interesting, lets do it, problem, no cash.'

'It's cheap, really, once we get down there you won't need much.' Better be right, I really was broke. The Air Force, great life style but little cash to finance it. A Eurail Pass, Phil said so, he's the source of all knowledge, likes organising, he's good at it, let the leader lead.

The cousins arrive, interesting, quite attractive, also from Canterbury, definitely country girls though. We set off in the train all the way to Brindisi on the heel of Italy, check into a cheap hotel and set ourselves up for a couple of days in the sun. The train was quite something, modern, all the facilities, comfortable, not at all like my childhood memories. Trains were smoky noisy things that rattled and bumped and when you went to the toilet you could see the train tracks flashing by right under the toilet bowl, disgusting. This was different, it didn't go clickity click either, just roared along. We left Germany, whizzed through Austria, then the full length of Italy, lovely, prosperous, green. As we got further south, it changed, became a bit brown looking, not so prosperous. Brindisi, lovely, plenty of cheap eating places around the old medieval harbour, and the wine was cheap. Cheap, cheap, this cheap business is starting to dominate, but we had no choice, the girls went along with it, wanted to stretch their money, only had so much to 'do Europe.' We got to know them during our Brindisi interlude, well I did, they were Phil's cousins, he'd known them all his life. They were good sorts. We took to sleeping in the one room, cheaper; 'now come on Phil, they're your cousins, of course I'll behave myself.' Evenings at the cafes by the harbour were magical, the sunsets, the wine, and the first of many tomato salads. The harbour was surrounded by a huge stone wall, a lovely sheltered place, impressive, and yes, the girls did get a couple of kisses, it was the wine, an excess of wine.

Next stop Corfu, I wanted to look up a place called Paleokastritsa. There's a Club Med there, or was, I think it may have been abandoned by now. One of the very first Club Meds, I had read about it somewhere. A couple of days on Corfu, 'how do we get there Phil?' He had it sussed, a vehicular ferry from Brindisi to Corfu. An enjoyable trip across the Adriatic, mostly Greeks and Italians, plus a few adventures from the other side of the world.

Beautiful place Corfu, monasteries, churches, they're everywhere, all very old. We find Paleokastritsa, a delightful little village by the sea, no Club Med, long gone, just a few derelict huts remained. I can imagine what it must have been in it's hey day, a real playground. A small pensione by a beach, just for us, two rooms this time. The mum and pop who ran it might balk at our one room habit, still cheap though and a great tomato and olive oil salad, perfect spot. Right on a beach, crystal clear water, warm, a taverna next door, everything we could possibly need.

We stayed there for four days, didn't move off the beach. The cousins were starting to give me a problem, kept turning out in ever smaller bikinis, suddenly they were not quite so horsy, but they were Phil's cousins, and Phil was my mate.

We went along to the local monastery, dated back to the thirteenth century. I had not seen anything like it before, impressive. Very religious the locals. Their monastery was the focal point of their lives, beautiful place, well maintained by the resident monks. All these icons, everywhere, dozens of them, and the candles, all alight, you took one, made a wish, then placed it in a little tray of sand, quite an experience. Far removed from anything we have in our part of the world. It heightened my awareness of what the old world was like.

Four days on the beach, time to move on, the girls put away their tiny bikinis and we're ready for the next stage of our journey to Crete.

'Phil, what's next?' quite happy to let him lead.

'There's a ferry to Piraeus, goes through the Corinth canal.'

The Corinth canal, that amazing piece of engineering from yesteryear. I'd read about it, now I was going to see it, sail through it, this will be fascinating. The ferry was big, will it fit, of course it will, dumb question, but when you see pictures of the canal it looks so narrow. They are deceptive, the canal is quite wide, big ships use it. The trip happens during the night. We're up on deck, it's an impressive sight, the walls on either side are high and the night sky is just a narrow strip way up above the boat, a full moon, visibility is good. We dock at Piraeus, two days in Athens, that's Phil's plan. I'm sure it will be good, it is.

The Acropolis, a 'must see.' We spend a whole day there, it's hot and there are hundreds of tourists doing the 'must see.' The place is huge, a great big pile of stones right in the centre of Athens, totally dominates the skyline. There are attendants with whistles that make a piercing noise if you get off the approved track, can be very embarrassing if you transgress. There seems to be a lot of whistle blowing, must be a lot of undisciplined tourists. I was to return to the Acropolis fifty years on, the whistle blowers were still evident. Fifty years, little had changed, even the toilets were the same, a hole in the floor, some western style ones had been added. Two days in Athens, still on tomato salads, and they still tasted good, those Mediterranean tomatoes really are tasty, how do they do it? Phil had been casting around for a boat to get us to Crete and during the evening 'tomato salad' on day one he advised us he'd found it, not the greatest, but affordable. The SS Angelika, forever burnt into my memory, the worst thing ever to float, a dunga, it gave new meaning to the word. Departs the day after tomorrow, one more day in Athens. More sightseeing, we've hardly scratched the surface, temples, ruins, the place is so old, so many leftovers from centuries ago; next morning, time to board.

'Cabins Phil?'

'Ah no, deck space only, there are cabins but they're outside the budget, besides it's warm, there's only one night involved, it'll be a new experience.'

'Yes Phil, if you say so.'

New experience indeed. The Angelika was a supply boat, the local tramp steamer, picked up and dropped off everything, literally everything, around the exotic Greek Islands. It's the boat the tourists don't see, would not want to see, but for some good keen adventurers from the antipodes, it's the one, cheap.

The deck cargo included us, lots of locals, rather poor locals, their chickens, goats, dogs, ducks, a lot of produce, sacks of potatoes, onions, all sorts of provisions piled up on the deck, different. The deck was very crowded, the sun was beating down, this might be difficult; it was.

'Come on, look on the bright side, this is a life experience, think of the tale we'll have to tell.'

I'm telling it now, definitely a oncer, would not be a starter for that again. We get to see the romantic Greek Islands from a different perspective, offloading and picking up at all the little ports on the islands, not the places where the cruise ships call, would not want the tourists to see the SS Angelika. I did not want to see it either but we were committed. It was fascinating, we were experiencing something that we would not have done had we been forewarned.

Eating? well what did you bring, there was no provision for eating on the boat. Good old Phil, he was onto it. We had stocked up in

Piraeus, a deck picnic with the goats, the pigs, the chickens, different!

When I reflect back on that boat trip, I have to admit, I was glad I did it, so unique, something you would never do by choice, but we did, it's just that we never realised just how basic life can be in some parts of the world. The night part, sleeping on deck with the livestock, and the locals. The girls were a bit nervous, not a problem, come in here under my blanket. Not the greatest. I had scrounged it off a bemused local, could not speak a word, no common language, but he got my drift, was only too happy to lend me his smelly blanket.

'I'll protect you, promise, you don't have to handcuff me?'
Quite an experience. It was warm, the stars were out, quite romantic. I was cuddled up with a cousin when a pig came and poked its nose in on us, talk about a turn off, ugh! There were chickens roaming around, small children, and the place smelt, an experience of the rather unpleasant kind.

Morning, a spectacular sunrise, one advantage of being up on deck. A beautiful morning, cruising amongst the fabulous Greek Islands, the place the tourist brochures go on about, and it was fabulous, as long as you did not cast your eye too closely over our 'cruise liner.' It was great, and cheap, it was the cheap bit that had landed us on this dunga. Great day, I lost track of where we went. There were numerous places and a lot of dropping off and picking up. The things the Angelika carried, there appeared to be no restrictions, anything and everything, the variety was endless. A lot of livestock, smelly livestock, and smelly locals. The deck became pretty dirty, there did not appear to be any effort to clean up after the livestock had fouled it. There was a hose and a fellow swished a bit of water around occasionally, that was it. There were drums of diesel, a lot of them, these were offloaded around the place and I got to thinking about just how dodgy the whole operation was. There was no provision for firefighting and there was a lot of diesel. There was the hose, that was it. Stop thinking about depressing things, enjoy the moment, one of life's experiences, a memory you can take to the grave. You'll never forget this boat trip and if you don't get off the Angelika soon you may go to your grave sooner rather than later. We arrive at Heraklion late in the afternoon, we're first off. I never want to see that dunga again, ever!

'Ah, well,' it's Phil, 'how can I put this, there's only the one boat that services Crete, the Angelika.'

'You're kidding me Phil, please say you're kidding me.'

'Not kidding, sorry.'

Phil looks concerned, I think he imagines he might have a rebellion on his hands.

'Phil, you've done well, you're a good organiser and we should be grateful, but g---z that boat's awful.'

'Ah, yes, you're not wrong there, sorry, I had no idea, life is a learning curve you know, we're learning.'

'Ok, forget the boat, lets find a taverna, I'm thirsty.'

Right on the waterfront, it takes guests as well, we check in. Two rooms, don't want to upset the locals with our communal approach, we can afford it; just. It's been an interesting journey getting here, now that we've arrived the place deserves a little of our time, there's a lot to see.

A beer, make that four, it's hot, the beer goes straight down, another four, and we start to relax. The taverna is nice and clean; after that boat we really appreciate the cleanliness. Several locals are eyeing us up; after a while one of them strikes up a conversation, his English is ok, a lot better than our Greek, well we did not speak any Greek, so his English was the only way we are going to communicate. After a bit it's apparent the locals do understand some

English but they're a bit reluctant to use it, they do get the drift of our conversation though and they're a friendly lot. We enjoy several beers then four ouzos arrive on the table. Where did this come from? A fellow along from us gives a bit of a wave and a huge smile, we smile back and raise the ouzo glasses in acknowledgment. It's terrible, ouzo, but hugely popular in Greece, an aniseed based liquor, definitely not my taste, but smile, down the hatch. The locals are a good lot, this could be a pleasant interlude here in Crete.

Getting hungry now, we order up some food, not tomato salads. There are lots of nice things on their menu. Very Greek, it's good, and cheap, so that problem goes away. We stay a long time in that taverna, eating, drinking, conversing, well sort of, with the friendly locals, this was a good place, that boat, that terrible boat, fast becoming just a bad memory, hang on, Phil said we were going to have to confront it again at some stage, b----r.

It's getting late, a great weariness is coming over me, probably the previous nights' lodgings has something to do with it. We'll settle our tab, then up to bed. There is no tab, must be, we've been here a long time, all that food and drink, no tab! This is embarrassing, then our English speaking friend explains in his limited English that the locals had settled our tab for us because we came from New Zealand. Kiwis are number one in Crete, they would be insulted if we did not allow them to do this. It was a hangover from the war. The New Zealand army had put up a stiff fight for Crete, the locals were not going to forget. Now we were embarrassed, this was far too generous, a drink or two perhaps, but a whole evening, and the food; that's the way it is our friend explained, the locals will be forever grateful for what your fathers did here, it'll never ever be forgotten. Well, not expected that, had not even given it a passing thought, had not given it a thought at all, in fact it became even more embarrassing when I realised just how scant my knowledge about that particular episode of the war was. Off to bed, a real bed, a good one, nice soft mattress, big eiderdown, Crete was shaping up as a good place.

Day two, 'we're going along to Knossos, it's not far.' This sounds interesting, Phil again, been doing his homework. Knossos rings a bell with me as well, I've read about it somewhere.

Breakfast at the Taverna, we're allowed to pay this time. The proprietor is overly attendant, seems we are the popular guests. Sightseeing today, Knossos, on the outskirts of Heraklion, a very old archaeological site, one of many on the island, probably the most famous. It's where the Minoan civilisation flourished during the Bronze Age two thousand years BC, the place where the Minatour, half man, half bull, used to live in Greek Mythology, in the labyrinth. It's where King Minos used to reign, an impressive site, there's a lot there. Some excellent restoration has been carried out. We spent an interesting day exploring the place, letting our imaginations roam, what would it have been like to have been around in those times. There are numerous throne rooms, we took photos of ourselves seated on a throne, King Minos's throne perhaps? I purchased a small Minoan vase, had to have a memento. It was late in the afternoon when we dragged ourselves away and returned to our taverna. It was a warm day, there was a beach close by and that's where we went, a bit of swimming and lying in the sun. That evening it was eating and drinking at the taverna, it seemed to be the best place around so why look elsewhere? This time we nailed the barman and arranged for the tab to be kept away from the locals, we would settle it. Another day on the beach, it was good swimming in the warm Aegean, then it was time to head north, our Mediterranean adventure was drawing to a close, but, and it was a big but, that boat, the SS Angelika, the only way out!

Grit the teeth, look at it this way, it's one of life's experiences, not a nice one but definitely an experience. On we get, nothing's changed, why would it? Not the sort of boat that's likely to see an upgrade anytime soon, if ever. It's a repeat of our previous trip, smelly locals, goats, pigs, rubbish, drums of diesel, gut wrenching stuff and I'm not feeling the greatest, find a piece of deck space and settle in. Back through the idyllic Aegean to Piraeus, it really was idyllic, it's just that the Angelika was so awful.

I've often thought about that trip to the Med so long ago, a lot of water has passed under the bridge since then, there have been quite a few cruises including a really good one on a boutique boat around the Greek Islands. How different when surrounded by all the creature comforts. Perhaps my sense of appreciation was heightened by that awful experience all those years ago.

Ephesus

'It's Kusadasi.'

'What?'

'Kusadasi, we're in Turkey. Come on, wake up, it's a new day and the sun's up. I think that French red got to you last night, no time for a hangover, we are about to enjoy an incredible experience, come on, smarten up.'

'Ah - yes, ok.'

We're on the Silver Wind, a boutique cruise boat, very comfortable, operating out of Venice, Silver Seas Line, a small family-owned Venetian shipping company. It had come to our attention back in New Zealand. We had booked a ten-day cruise, Venice to Istanbul.

'Come on, get with it, Kusadasi, we're in Turkey.'
All new to me, I had not even heard of the place but I was suffering from information overload. We had been on this boat for five days, thoroughly pampered, subjected to a new experience every day. I had not caught up. To-day it's Kusadasi and Ephesus, 'excuse me, Ephesus?' I was about to discover one of the wonders of the ancient world and I did not know a thing about it, not even the name.

Breakfast on our private balcony, into the shower, prepare for another day of sightseeing. We've done a lot of sightseeing and the sights have been fabulous, Corfu, Santorini, Mykonus, plenty more to come. We're travelling with another couple; we'd learnt long ago that cruises are more fun if you take your own company.

Assemble in the lobby, down the gangplank, onto our bus, got the right one? Several tours are on offer, there are a lot of busses. We 'had the word' there was only the one, Ephesus. Cameras ready. I had my handycam, I liked to think I made great home movies, the girls had their little still cameras, 'take plenty of pictures, we'll cull them later.'

Off through Kusadasi, a surprisingly large city, and I never knew it existed. We were down in the bottom left-hand corner of Turkey, if you look at a map, there it is; it's just that I had never looked. Through the town and up into the hinterland. We are going to Mary's house. Virgin Mary of biblical fame. Must have got around that Mary, she pops up all over the Mediterranean and one of these places is a hilltop in behind Kusadasi. We arrive at a lovely spot high up on a mountain, Mary's house, all alone in an olive grove. A little old stone structure, quite impressive. A rather incongruous note, a young Turkish policeman armed with a machine gun standing in what looks like some kind of bunker. Coming from New Zealand we find the approach to security in this part of the world very different. We are allowed into Mary's house in small groups, no cameras, and please be quiet. The place has a certain 'aura,' dark and quiet, a lot of lighted candles. There's a small shrine where you can place a candle and make a wish. Outside, a long wishing wall covered in pieces of paper, thousands of pieces of paper. The idea is to make a wish and attach it to the wall. On a slightly elevated site nearby an open-air church service, the singing adds to the atmosphere. Mary certainly selected a lovely spot for her house. Back onto the bus, now the main event, Ephesus but before I begin, a little history.

Present day Ephesus is a small part of what was once a very large city, there's a vast area yet to be rediscovered. Human habitation dates back almost eight thousand years. Originally a Greek city called Anatolia, founded around one thousand BC, it was taken over by the Romans during the first century BC and developed into one of the major cities in the ancient Mediterranean with a population of around a quarter of a million people. The Romans built some impressive structures including one of the seven wonders of the ancient world, the Temple of Artemis. Ephesus prospered for several centuries then a series of events conspired to bring about its gradual decline. The harbour, a major factor in the city's success, silted up, malaria, civil insurrection, a series of invasions, and a severe earthquake, hastened the decline. By six hundred AD it was all over for Ephesus, the once grand city was then just a small village.

To-day it's a major archaeological site, probably the most significant one in the old Roman Empire. About 15% of the original city has been excavated and this alone covers a huge area, just how big this project will eventually become is an open question, and a very exciting one for the archaeologists. There are some notable structures, the Library of Celsius is probably the most impressive. There's the Temple of Hadrian, and sections of what was a very advanced aqueduct system. A huge outdoor amphitheatre, the largest in the ancient world, it seated twenty-four thousand. Endless other minor structures and never-ending piles of old stone columns and blocks. Ephesus is also the site of a major gladiator graveyard discovered relatively recently. A photographer's heaven, the light is perfect, the subject matter endless. We took countless pictures; the eventual culling process will be long and difficult.

Our tour guide was excellent, great sense of humour and very knowledgeable. He carried a bright blue umbrella that he used as a sunshade, good idea the sun was fierce and the brolly was an unmistakable rallying point for our rather large group.

The tour of the archaeological site started at the head of a valley. There was an area of flat land and a small amphitheatre, a lot of stone blocks, the remains of toppled columns, and plenty of carved figures and friezes just lying about in apparent disarray. From there we proceeded down the valley, a spectacular sight. It had once been a grand avenue lined with temples, fountains and numerous statues. As we progressed further down the valley the Library of Celsius came into view, spectacular, it dominated the area. We spent some time at the library, it was the focal point of the excavation, very impressive.

A lot of the structures were scarred with what appeared to be big bullet holes, however, there was a pattern to the holes, not the random scatter you would expect. A query to our guide brought forth a fascinating tale.

The Eastern Mediterranean has been troubled by piracy for centuries, even back in Roman times. The coast of southern Turkey has always been a hot spot. When the ancients erected their stone columns they developed a system of iron rod reinforcement to hold the blocks in alignment and give some protection against earthquakes, a problem was the iron corroding. To prevent this they poured molten lead into the holes containing the rods and thus protect them from corrosion. When the musket came along centuries later the pirates of the time, requiring lead for their musket balls, discovered a plentiful supply in the old ruins at Ephesus. They bored holes into the joints between the stone blocks, applied heat, and extracted the lead, it was these holes we were seeing.

Numerous stray cats frequented the place. There was 'boss cat,' a big scarred fellow with ragged ears and a mean disposition. It was noticeable how the lesser felines scattered when this fellow appeared.

An ancient public toilet, this was a surprise, different and quite unexpected. Ephesus was blessed with a good water supply and the Romans had built an excellent public toilet system supplied by an aqueduct, another of the engineering wonders to be found at Ephesus. There was this well-restored public toilet, a long marble bench with suitable cut-outs to accommodate a customer's backside, below this a deep channel flushed with constant running water, I was impressed, we took a lot of pictures.

When we did the tour there were hundreds, probably thousands of tourists, the place was awash with humanity but because it's so big this was not a problem, our guide's bright blue umbrella was definitely a good idea. From the main excavation we moved on to a museum containing some real treasures that had been recovered from the site, it was fascinating. These small, and some not so small, statues and figures were quite incredible in their intricacy and beauty, they were all housed in controlled conditions in a museum to ensure their future survivability. Something that you could not help but notice was the apparent fascination the Romans had for male genitalia, many of the carvings were quite explicit in this area.

All this picture taking used up my last couple of films, what to do, where can I get some film? Surprise, there were some shops by the museum and they had the very film I wanted, another surprise, the price was right.

We had 'done' Ephesus, very impressive, we reboarded our bus, hang on, is it ours? there were dozens of them lined up in the parking area. 'Yep, it's ours, there's the blue brolly.' We set off back to Kusadasi, mid-afternoon, very hot. We were basking in all our newfound knowledge. I strongly recommend to anyone who may find themselves in the south west part of Turkey, visit this place, well worth the effort. A refreshment stop, part of the tour package, and another surprise. A spectacular cliff top hotel looking out over the Aegean Sea where we enjoyed an excellent Turkish smorgasbord and unlimited Efas beer, the local drop, and rather good. The huge high-ceilinged air-conditioned dining room enjoyed a spectacular view and the food was excellent, a fitting end to what had been an excellent day's sightseeing. Back to our comfortable boat, what does to-morrow have in store?

Dubai

'Aaahhh! Eeehh,' the girls are screaming in the back. We've just crested a sand dune and are hurtling down its far side in a four-wheel drive. We're out in the desert having a 'desert experience.' It starts with a hair-raising drive amongst some seriously big sand dunes, real 'on the edge' stuff.

What are we doing in Dubai? We're on our way to Athens, a wedding in Greece, a Kiwi girl, a relative, is marrying a young Greek chap in a hilltop village near Missolonghi, a three-hour drive from Athens; this could be interesting. These days if you want to get to the Mediterranean from New Zealand you fly directly there, no going via Europe. We are flying to Athens, with a stop at Dubai, the stopover of choice. We plan on spending a few days here and taking in all it has to offer. There are four of us, two couples. One of the girls has taken it upon herself to organise the whole thing, so far, she's doing well. Right now she's in the back seat screaming; *'having a wonderful time.'*

We left Auckland four days ago, September, a surprisingly good day when we left. It's meant to be cold wet and windy when you escape from winter, well it wasn't. We flew to Dubai in a big jet, a very big jet, first time I had been in one, but it still took forever. Dubai, very hot, huge airport terminal, and I mean huge, along to the Pullman Hotel in the Avenue of the Sheiks, dog tired but no resting, we have a full schedule. Quick scrub up, brief lie down, then psyche ourselves for a unique experience, *'high tea at the Burj Al Arab.'* You have probably seen pictures of a spectacular high rise in Dubai shaped like a huge sail, that's the Burj Al Arab, and way up near the top there's a cigar shaped appendage, that's a restaurant, a very good restaurant, one of the best in the world, we are going up there to have high tea.

'Really! Looks expensive.'

'Yep, you're not wrong.'

'How expensive?'

'You don't want to know.'

It's all prepaid. We get a taxi and front the causeway leading to the Burj. It's on an artificial island and access is restricted. We have to produce tickets for our high tea before we're allowed across. We arrive, what a sight, the building is huge, quite unlike anything I have ever seen, space age. Outside are three courtesy cars, matching white Rolls Royce Phantoms. In we go, again I'm blown away, the architecture is spectacular. You have to put this place on your bucket list. We admire the huge atrium, twenty stories high at least, fountains, tropical aquariums, gardens, there's just so much in this place, it takes a while to adjust the mind to the sheer splendour of it all. The elevator whisks us silently up to the stratosphere, to one of the world's great restaurants, the view out across the water is sensational. Way down below there's a marina, multi-million dollar boats, yachts I guess is the trendy term, but really, they are huge powerboats, small ships. Not far away is another spectacular building, the Dubai Hilton with a huge manicured white sand beach in front of it, beach umbrellas all lined up in neat rows, beach attendants very much in evidence. This is the absolute top end of the market, I was impressed. High tea, champagne for openers, Dom Perignon, the best. Our waiter puts on an impressive display pouring it, he knows his stuff, again I'm impressed. If this keeps up I am going to be wandering around Dubai in a state of continuous impressedness! Is there such a word? A selection of small cakes, canapés, sandwiches, all sorts of nice things, presented on a small silver tower tray shaped like the Burj, accompanied by a tea menu, an elegant listing of fifty different teas that are available; 'please make your selection and your choice will be prepared specifically to that tea producer's specifications.' I peruse the list, none of them are familiar, I enlist the help of our waiter. He knows everything and is familiar with my dilemma, it happens all the time. A tea is decided on and it arrives on a silver serving trolly, cups, teapot, hot water, napkins, everything required to make tea. Instructions are given about how long the tea needs to brew etc, and 'a little more champagne perhaps.' 'Would you like me to make it for you sir?' The whole high tea experience is enthralling, a unique experience, the tea itself, extraordinary. During 'tea' a grand piano plays discretely in the background, just perfect.

We remain in the dining room for some time, it's so enjoyable. Eventually it's the ultra smooth elevator back to the lobby where we again marvel at the sheer luxury of the place. Out into the heat of the afternoon and a taxi back to the Pullman. Perhaps a short lie down, then it'll be cocktail time. Day one, great so far.

Day two, Dubai creek, a market area that specialises in gold, and you can buy *real* fake watches. The gold shops are incredible, there's some extraordinary gold jewellery on display. The girls become very interested. 'Wow there girls, we're from New Zealand, remember.' A fake watch perhaps, have to buy something. 'Very good fake watches sir,' the salesman is persistent, he succeeds; eventually. Several walkouts, throwaway offers, then a sale. I weaken and purchase a very smart Rolex. It's ridiculously cheap! lasted three days, but it was an experience.

That evening a dinner cruise on Dubai Creek, another *must do,* superb. Three hours on a dhow set up as a floating restaurant. We cruised along Dubai Creek and enjoyed a magnificent Oriental meal, Arabian music playing discretely in the background, another unforgettable experience.

Day three, we're out in the desert. There's a lot of screaming from the back seat and my heartbeat is off the clock. Another couple of *vertical* sandhills and we stop for a photo op. Then it's camel riding time, hilarious, hunting with falcons, amazing, then a desert feast, the highlight of the day.

Several separate tour groups come together for this evening event. We're spread out on huge rugs under some date palms, a selection of Arabian food to die for. The girls get the backs of their hands decorated with quite exotic wax tattooing. I guess hand washing is off for a while, then it's belly dancing, a really good show. It went on far into the night, we were in fantasy land, Arabian Nights.

Everything about Dubai is impressive, the enormous wealth was obvious, gouged from the petrol pumps of the world. The Burg Khalifa, tallest tower in the world, 830 meters, twice the height of the Eiffel Tower, 1.5 billion dollars to build. We take the high-speed elevator to the observation deck on floor 148, 535 meters up. The view is mind blowing. Down in the atrium there's a vending machine that sells gold bars, genuine gold bullion bars, you use a credit card. There's an aquarium, a Kelly Tarlton copy, it's good, and shopping malls catering to the top end of the market; the wealth in this place is incredible. But there's something missing, there's nothing old, everything's new and shiny, new money, no real history. Oil had created Dubai and the enormous wealth extorted from the rest of the world is concentrated in the hands of the Sheiks who control the place. I'm just envious; Dubai certainly is an extreme example of what real wealth can create.

Our schedule, yes, we do have a plan for our trip to Greece. It has us flying out of Dubai for Istanbul, it'll be very different to Dubai, very old, shrouded in history going way back, nothing *nouveau riche* about Istanbul.

Incident In Hong Kong

'Captain, there's a problem.'
This unwelcome message awoke me from an alcohol induced sleep in a hotel room in Hong Kong early one morning.
'What's that? a problem?'
I tried valiantly to assemble my thoughts. It had been a late knight in Joe's bar, a well-known watering hole in Cameron Road deep in the bowels of Tsim Sha Tsui, now, unfortunately, long gone.
'I'm not in the best shape right now to handle problems, what is it?'
It was the Chief Purser, he sounded concerned.
'One of our hostesses was mugged last knight, purse stolen, she was knocked about a bit.'
Suddenly I'm wide awake, this could really be a problem.

Apparently one of our hostesses had disembarked from a Star Ferry late the previous evening and been accosted by one of the rickshaw boys who frequent the ferry terminal area. A middle-aged chap with a 'bad disposition.' When our girl declined his forceful offer to take her somewhere in his rickshaw he had whacked her, grabbed her handbag, and disappeared. The distraught girl had made it to the hotel on foot, it's not far from the ferry terminal, and contacted our Chief Purser. It became a police matter very quickly. The rickshaw fellow was apprehended in no time at all, handbag recovered. There's to be a court appearance later that day, they don't muck around in Hong Kong, and they really don't like visitors being attacked. The Chief Purser was going along to the court with our hostess, he was inquiring if I would like to be there as well.

'Of course I want to be there.'

The poor girl will need all the support she can get. Quite apart from the seriousness of the situation it could be interesting; it was. Straight out of a Dickens novel. A judge, in full regalia, wig, robes, the lot, high on a pedestal, towering above everything, and a thoroughly broken little man in chains in the dock way below, well that's how my imagination saw it, made me think, it must have been like this in 'yesteryear.' Transportation to the colonies or hanging. It was short and sharp. Our girl, our upset girl, was required to say a few words, there did not appear to be any provision for defence. The heinous criminal with murderous intent was dispatched straight to jail. That was it, all over, outside into the late morning sunshine, coffee shop, our hostess needed a bit of looking after. Good work story when she gets home!

Lest We Forget

They shall not grow old as we that are left grow old, age shall not weary them nor the years condemn, at the going down of the sun, and in the morning, we will remember them, we will remember them.

I choked up, tears came to my eyes, it never occurred to me I might react this way. We were at Lone Pine, a war cemetery high above ANZAC Cove on the Gallipoli Peninsular, the emotion of the place really got to me. Down by the beach there were a lot of Kiwi graves, we visited them earlier in the day, it was while we were there that I felt this change coming over me. Up at Lone Pine the full impact of what had happened here hit home, twelve thousand young men *from the uttermost ends of the earth* had died at this place. Laurence Binyon's famous Ode of Remembrance just entered my mind.

We were doing the Gallipoli pilgrimage, a rite of passage for Kiwis in recent years; it was a moving experience. It came about because of a wedding in Greece. A young New Zealand relative had married a fellow from a small Greek village, we had gone to the wedding. That was something else as well, another story there. Because we had traveled all this way, we added a car trip around southern Greece and a Mediterranean Cruise. Our cruise ship stopped at Çanakkale in the Dardanelles, the jumping off point for the Gallipoli battlefields; several tours were on offer. We bought into one back in New Zealand. The guide was an interesting fellow, an internationally known commentator on the Gallipoli campaign.

Our tour took us along the waterfront at Çanakkale, onto a vehicular ferry, then across the Dardanelles Strait to Eceabat on the Gallipoli Peninsular. It was here where Alexander the Great crossed the Hellespont with ninety thousand men two thousand years earlier. Then across the peninsular to the western side, and ANZAC Cove, Koyu Beach. The sight of the beach, and the New Zealand cemetery behind it, brought a lump to my throat. I'd been hearing about this place all my life, now here I was in my retirement years finally seeing it, why had it taken so long? I don't know. I had been to Turkey. The Big OE was all the rage way back in the 1950s. At that time the events that transpired at Gallipoli were not well known to the younger generation, the Second World War was the dominant event in our lives. In more recent years there's been a remarkable resurgence of interest about what happened here in the Dardanelles in 1915. The Gallipoli battlefields have become a place of pilgrimage for people from our part of the world. It was a moving experience, brought tears to my eyes; that surprised me.

We wandered along the stony beach at ANZAC cove and the small cemetery just above. A lot of headstones, all neat and tidy, a lot of red carnations, neatly trimmed lawns and gardens, someone looked after this place, that was nice. The inscriptions on the headstones were quite moving, these soldiers were so young when they met their violent ends. I picked up a pebble from the beach, a small piece of marble, brought it home. This small stone would have been witness to the terrible events which took place here, I just felt I had to have something tangible, a part of our heritage. Just off the beach a local fishing boat was trolling lures. I watched them pull in an Albacore Tuna the same species we catch in New Zealand, that really put a lump in my throat.

Looking up at the hills behind the beach, the hills those soldiers had been confronted with, you realize the impossibility of the task. Little cover, steep terrain, and an enemy dug in on the high ground. It's understandable why the casualty count was so high, and it was very high, one in four of the Kiwis who landed at ANZAC cove died on the peninsular. I stood for a long time looking up at those hills trying to imagine it all, it was not very nice. The sheer impossibility of getting up there in the face of heavy gunfire from a very capable adversary commanded by a brilliant military man, Ataturk. Churchill got it wrong when he pitted the Allies against that man. Ataturk went on to create the modern Turkish state from the ashes of the Ottoman Empire. He is a revered figure in that country to this day. He also coined the expression, *'from the uttermost ends of the earth.'* It appears on several Turkish memorials to the ANZACs that are in the area. Ataturk had a great admiration for the fighting ability of the ANZAC troops.

We spent some time at the beach, took some pictures. There were four of us from Auckland. We were taking the sort of photos the grandchildren might treasure, *'the olds at ANZAC Cove.'* Then we re-boarded our bus and went up into those foreboding hills, to Lone Pine, where I had more trouble with my emotions. Lone Pine is impressive. Built by the Australians to commemorate their 9,000 dead and New Zealand's 3000. There are hundreds of headstones arranged in a huge square, a solitary pine tree brought from Melbourne. At one end there's a big stone memorial inscribed with hundreds of names from our part of the world, all killed in the area, such enormous loss of life from a couple of countries that did not have all that many people to start with; *'from the uttermost ends of the earth,'* the words are burnt into my memory. There were some Australians in our group and the raw emotion that the place stirred up was quite noticeable amongst them, such a waste of life.

Back on the bus, along to Chunuk Bair, a place where New Zealand suffered huge losses and earned a Victoria Cross. This was the farthest point of the Allied advance on the Gallipoli Peninsular, almost in sight of the Dardanelles, a place the New Zealanders never managed to actually see before being routed by Ataturk's massed forces. There are several monuments at Chunuk Bair, more New Zealand names. Nearby there's a big Turkish cemetery and memorial park, the Turks lost many thousands in this area. The fighting at

Chunuk Bair was some of the fiercest of the campaign. From the heights you could look back down the steep slopes to ANZAC Cove, it appeared to be a long way away. It's remarkable that the Allies managed to get this far before being driven back, so close to the ultimate objective, which was to take and hold the high ground on the peninsular.

We spent some time at Chanuk Bair letting our imaginations wander. We encountered a young Turkish couple; they were amazed that we came from New Zealand. Apparently the locals have a lot of respect for the ANZACs from yesteryear. This young couple could not believe we had traveled all the way from New Zealand to be at this place.

It was now midafternoon, Chanuk Bair marked the end of our tour. We boarded our bus, went back to Eceabat and across the Dardanelles Strait to Çanakkali, it was all over. We were a subdued group; it had been a sobering few hours. Those casualty figures, they were huge. It's not generally known just how horrendous they really were. The Allies lost almost as many men as the Turks in the Gallipoli campaign, the British alone lost 34,000 killed, the French 10,000, around 55,000 allied soldiers were killed. It's hard to determine how many Turkish soldiers lost their lives but the best estimates put the number around 87,000, but then casualty numbers during the First World War were so appalling it becomes a bit hard to comprehend. To us in New Zealand it was the fact that we lost so many, one in four, from a small country that did not have many young men to start with.

Earlier, when we had driven across the peninsular, we stopped at a local farmhouse. The family who farmed the area had been doing so for generations. In the years following the war they were constantly finding the things war leaves behind, just lying around. They started a small museum to display these items. Today this has grown into a remarkable collection of all the things that an army takes with it into battle. Dozens of old rusty rifles, bayonets, hand grenades, artillery shells of every size and shape, the remains of gun carriages, broken wheels, steel helmets, water bottles, handguns, a good collection of old maps and charts, the remains of uniforms, boots, belts, it just went on and on. All these things were battered and in poor condition. When you think about what they had endured, this was not surprising. Looking at these things mentally prepared us for the unexpected emotions we experienced when we actually arrived at ANZAC Cove, went up into those hills behind, Lone Pine, Chanuk Bair.

Down by the beach at ANZAC Cove there is a large stone memorial engraved with a moving eulogy to the ANZACs from Ataturk. It is dated 1934. Ataturk had a tremendous admiration for our fighting men and his eulogy is quite remarkable, very humbling, it hints at the futility of war.

It had been an emotionally charged day for us, certainly for me, I was glad we had come to this place, we had done the pilgrimage.

From the uttermost ends of the earth
Lest we forget.

Sitoko

'Sitoko,'

'Lynette.'

It's an exuberant exchange, four years in the making. Osaka airport. We had just arrived from Auckland, the culmination of a long-planned visit to see Sitoko, and meet her parents. She had been to New Zealand several times, an English language exchange student, had stayed with her 'New Zealand family' on each occasion. Sitoko was now an attractive young woman quite grown up from the shy fourteen-year old who first visited us six years earlier. She was crying, an emotional girl, the tears were flowing, she was so happy to see us.

'My father Masaki, and my mother Sako.'

Both had big smiles and nodded, no English, well we had no Japanese, Sitoko will be busy. Fortunately her English is excellent. She had been suggesting this trip for some time, now here we are, our first time in Japan. We had been to Asia several times, but not Japan. Here for a week, staying with Sitoko's family; this will be different. An awkward interval then Sitoko takes over.

'Now we will go and get the car and go for lunch.'

'Sitoko is there an ATM, I need some yen.'

'Ah, this way, there's an international ATM, you will have to do it here at the airport, it's the only place where you can get yen with a foreign card. The ATMs here are different to New Zealand,' Sitoko tells us.

Transaction completed, we're off in the family car. It's a 'people mover,' accommodates nine. There's another couple in the group, Sitoko's older brother and his girlfriend, again, no English.

It's an impressive place, a traditional 'picture postcard' Japanese restaurant, but this is real, this is the way the Japanese do it. A beautiful garden, running water, bamboo screens, low tables, beautifully dressed waitresses, and I have absolutely no idea about what I am supposed to eat or drink, way outside my comfort zone, but it certainly looks interesting. It would appear that Masaki has taken us to an exclusive restaurant, very Japanese, not a European in sight. There is some discussion between Sitoko and her dad, we gather it's about what we might, and might not, like to eat. Just as well Sitoko has taken over because, as I said, I am way out of my depth here. The meal is a revelation, endless dishes arrive, every one absolutely delicious, no idea what they are, but I like them all.

This lunch sets the tone for our visit, Masaki kept taking us to all these excellent restaurants, places we would never otherwise have experienced, would not have known where to go, or what to do. Masaki insisted on paying for everything and his generosity became embarrassing, these restaurants were not cheap. Sitoko explained, 'it's the Japanese way.' Masaki would be offended if we did not allow him to do this. But it did not stop with restaurants, there was white water rafting, I think that was expensive, numerous temples, huge wooden affairs hundreds of years old, shrines, castles, old buildings, Masaki had his hand in his pocket constantly. He was a fireman, a senior officer at the local fire station in their village, Wakayama, near Osaka. He had a T shirt with the wording 'I Survived The Kobe Earthquake' printed on it. This T shirt was significant, Masaki was deeply involved in that terrible event in 1995.

It just got better; we were seeing a Japan I don't think we would have encountered otherwise. Staying with Sitoko's family was a whole new experience. The house shoes, sleeping on the floor, the near vertical stairs, the little electric lift, the movable wall screens. Masaki's other occupation, rice growing. He had little plots of rice all around the village that he harvested, processed, packaged, and sold. There was a shed full of machinery specifically for dealing with rice. And the eating; quite apart from all the restaurants, the meals that Sako prepared at home were fantastic. Sitting on the floor, cooking at the low table, so very different, so enjoyable, then suddenly, it was all over, well not quite!

There was a boyfriend, Yusoki, and during the course of our stay Sitoko confided in us that it was their intention to come to New Zealand in a year's time to get married, she wanted to include her 'New Zealand family.'

More visits to big old wooden castles, shrines, Shinto and Buddhist temples, some going back a thousand years. A lot of history, something people from New Zealand are not familiar with. Then it was over, back to New Zealand but we'll see our 'Japanese family' again, they are planning a visit to Auckland for Sitoko and Yusoki's wedding.

Wahoo, Bourbon, & Prawns

'*Four cases*,' the first words to the ground engineer. He's just plugged into the intercom's external jack point. We're at Pago Pago, American Samoa, it's early morning, a quick turn 'round then we'll be winging our way back to Nadi in Fiji. Four cases of Wahoo, forty-eight tins in a case, best value in town. The ground engineer's the contact, takes the order, dispatches his man to the local supplier, adds his 'fee,' and delivers the goods, all in quick time, an excellent service, very popular, unbelievable value, the stuff is so cheap.

The Wahoo run, that's what it's called, a regular TEAL service between Auckland and Pago Pago, via Nadi. We'll arrive back in Auckland with all this canned fish; Customs hate it. Fish was exempt from any customs restrictions. This went right against their mind set.

The 1960s, New Zealand was a 'can't have' place, everything was subject to customs duty or banned completely, except fish. We exploited this loophole, did not gain us any friends with Customs, they were anti on principle.

Wahoo, it's a tuna species found in abundance in the Pacific. There's a big American fishing operation in Pago Pago, a big cannery, and some willing buyers from New Zealand who turn up early in the morning in their own aeroplane, sometimes with quite substantial orders.

TEAL, Tasman Empire Airways Limited, forerunner of Air New Zealand, operated a fleet of Lockheed Electras, a big turbo prop passenger aeroplane. Across the Tasman and around the South Pacific. I was a very young Electra Captain, did the wahoo run frequently. Everyone and everything ate wahoo. A delightful snack, so ridiculously cheap, just a few cents a can; cats loved it. I was going through the 'pet cat' phase of my life, wahoo, flown in from Pago Pago, featured large on their menu.

The other popular purchase at Pago, bourbon. I'm not a bourbon drinker but the fancy bottles it came in, real collector's items and again, cheap. The bottles could be utilised as gifts, they really were quite unique, or heaven forbid, as candle holders. The bourbon inside? well our guests were always overindulged with bourbon and coke, got to empty the bottle, I need it; empty.

The return flight to Nadi included an interesting bit of flying that our passengers loved. Viti Levu, Fiji's main Island, is dissected by some very big canyons, they are orientated east west, the same direction as our flight path. We would fly the last part of the flight right down low along one of these canyons. The passengers were presented with a spectacular sight, bush clad cliffs towering above on both sides of the aircraft, they loved it and I loved doing it, great fun. It also allowed an abbreviated approach at Nadi airfield that saved the company some fuel.

The wahoo popped up all over the place in Auckland, the word was out, 'any chance of a case of wahoo?' It was not just the price, the stuff was absolutely delicious, could be used in so many different ways. The cats? well it was cheaper than cat food and the cats loved it, how many cases can a person bring home?

There was another 'fish flight,' the prawn run, Sydney to Auckland. Prawns were virtually unknown in New Zealand, they came from Sydney and were expensive, an import monopoly, a real rort, common in New Zealand in the 60s. Different these days, everything's available, but not then. Fresh prawns were common in Sydney, and cheap. A traditional Australian delicacy, something that was popular with me. TEAL operated a daily service between

Sydney and Auckland, sometimes twice a day. We had this fish shop out by Mascot Airport organised. The idea was to assemble an order for fresh prawns from amongst the crew, phone it through to the fish shop, and pick it up on the way to the airport. Had to get the Chief Purser in on the act. The prawns had to be chilled during the flight, that's where he came in, he ran the galleys and fridges. The arrangement worked well, the fish shop loved us, they got some substantial orders. Customs were beside themselves, the very idea of us being able to bring in fresh prawns, unencumbered by customs restrictions, got right up their noses, strange lot those Customs people.

There was a downside to our 'fish importing.' When we did bring home something that *was* subject to duty, Customs nailed us, sometimes quite unjustifiably, but when you think it through, I guess we brought it upon ourselves, we did push the fish thing.

Today it's completely different, you can bring just about anything into New Zealand, all the liquor you could possibly need, Customs are not interested, but drugs, that's a different story, that's where all the effort is directed, should have been like that years ago.

I see wahoo's on the supermarket shelf these days and there are plenty of Australian prawns in the supermarket freezer, the world has changed!

A Wedding In Stamna

'Kirsty's getting married!'
'You're kidding.'
'Not kidding, she's fallen for a Greek chap, it's serious.'
'There's going to be a wedding, in Stamna.'
'Where?'
'Stamna.'
'Where in the world is Stamna?'
'On a hilltop just north of Missolonghi, it's a little village.'
'Missolonghi?
'In Greece.'
'Greece?'
'Yep.'

Well that caused a stir, atlas, maps, Google Earth, where in the world is Missolonghi? where's Stamna? and what's with the Greek chap?
'We're invited?'
'Hmm, that's a long way to go, when is it?'
'In three months.'
'Hmm, different, could be good, long way though. We've not got anything planned for this year, would need to flesh it out a bit, make all that travel worthwhile.'
'Who will be going?'
'Perhaps the two of us and I think sis and hubby would be on for it, what about bro? he's going to Europe about then, Italy I think, visiting the rellies, could be interested.'
'We should give it some serious thought, could take in Greece, the Med, make it worthwhile, what do you think?'
'The idea appeals, never been to Greece.'

'We'll call Lita and Nigel, find out what their globetrotting daughter is up to, I guess they will be going, father of the bride, he pays doesn't he?'

'We are going, sis and hubby are on for it as well, bro's not sure.' These decisions were arrived at quite quickly, going to Greece had appeal. Never really been there, passed through once when I was on the big OE, but that was a long time ago.
'Sis, you like organizing trips, you're good at it, how about this one?'
'Err, ok, where do we want to go?'

It took off from there, developed a life of its own. A trip around Greece, rental car, places you don't know a thing about, Kyparissia, Corinth, Kalamata, and a couple of places that do ring a bell, Olympia, Delphi, Patras, then there's getting there? The way to do it is via the Middle East, forget America, transiting Los Angeles has killed that one. Dubai's the place, spend some time there, everyone says it's great. Perhaps a cruise, the eastern Med, what about it sis? Sis, my partner's sister, has the travel bug, done a lot of it, knows the ropes so leave it to someone who knows what they're doing. In no time at all things are falling into place, a few days in Dubai, a few more in Athens, rental car around the southern part of Greece, take in some ancient sites, Olympia and Delphi in particular, the wedding, then fly to Venice. A cruise around the Med. It's getting to sound really good.

It's happening, we're in Stamna, inside a church, an incredibly ornate church, lots of gold, very colourful, religious icons and paintings, a high vaulted ceiling, lots of decoration, Greek orthodox, very different.
Kirsty and her man, her 'about to be' Greek husband; far removed

from the image we had in our minds. Kirsty's a vivacious girl, attractive. We thought she would have found *a hunk,* but no, quite the opposite, a small quiet intellectual fellow. It's obvious Kirsty loves him, that's nice, it's just that we are having trouble getting our heads around her choice, oh well perhaps it's a generational thing, young people are different, every generation is different, perhaps we need to get with it!

A Greek orthodox wedding. The church is packed, relatives from far and wide, *even people from New Zealand.* The bride and groom up at the alter before an imposing priest, full regalia, very colourful. He starts off on a long dissertation that we cannot follow, not sure about the language, Latin perhaps, I ask a girl standing nearby, 'do you speak English?' 'Yes, I do,' 'what's the language, Latin?' The girl is a character and tells us she has no idea what the priest is on about or what the language is, neither does anybody else, these priests take centre stage at events like this, give long dissertations that nobody understands, but it's entertaining. Eventually the priest runs out of words, there's some action. Small crowns, Stephana, are placed on the bride and groom's heads, some exchanging of crowns, some walking around the alter holding candles and sipping wine from a cup, rings are exchanged and placed on the right hand, different. Then he's off again. The priest launches into another long dissertation that no one understands. There are some elderly fellows sitting behind the alter, church elders who always attend these events. It's interesting, they appear to be asleep, understandable, the priest's long ramblings in the not understandable language was very conducive to sleep. The priest finishes, there's some laying on of hands on a big book accompanied by the swinging of small incense burning gourds, and suddenly it's all over.

Out into the bright sunlight, a milling crowd, a big limo, and the happy couple are off. There's to be a reception at a place down the hill after the mandatory photos have been taken. Kirsty's now married *to a Greek!*

Heinlager or Steineken,

'Excuse me?'

'Heinlager or Steineken, you heard.'

'What are you talking about, you've been drinking!'

'Yep, true, and you're hard of hearing. I said Heinlager or Steineken, what's it to be?'

'Never heard of them, I think you're a bit confused.'

'No, those are the choices, look, it's right here.'

Two bottles were produced, one had a Heineken label and a Steinlager cap, and the other a Steinlager label and a Heineken cap; what gives?

What indeed? We were in the garden bar at an up-market resort at Muri beach in Rarotonga when we were confronted with this conundrum. I had noticed a similar bottle the day before but had disregarded it, too much to drink, after all we were on holiday, the sun was beating down, and everything in the world was perfect, well not quite, there appeared to be a problem with the beer. My preference is Heineken, I don't particularly like Steinlager, so it was necessary to be specific when ordering a beer. There were four of us beer drinkers, the girls had found a shop, would not see them for a while.

'So, what's going on with the beer?'

We examined the two bottles, looked normal, except for the unique labelling, or was it the unique caps? Needs investigating, we opened them and drank.

'Can you tell what it is?'

'How about you?'

The consensus was that neither tasted true to label, so what were they? Numerous possibilities came to mind. Our best guess was that there was a mixture of beers in both bottles, so how had that happened? This was supposed to be a good hotel, surely they would not be short changing us with the beer, what's the explanation? We went inside and eyeballed all the bottles we could see, nothing appeared amiss and the barman was giving us a suspicious look. We decided not to press the matter, don't rock the boat, it's lovely here, but keep a close eye on the beer.

The two suspect bottles had been purchased at the bar. The service out in the garden had been a bit slow, normally the beer came already poured, you never got to see the bottle. Having downed the two unusual ones we caught the attention of the waiter and ordered another two Heinekens, and two Steinlagers; 'please bring them unopened.' They duly arrived and there was nothing untoward about the labelling. We opened them, they were as advertised. Well now the great beer mystery.

The next couple of hours were spent sitting in the sunshine in the garden bar debating the endless possibilities. Imaginations ran riot, all sorts of explanations surfaced, most of them involving some sort of shady practice. Our waiter could not figure out why we were insisting that he bring the numerous bottles of beer we were downing, in the bottle, unopened, we were not about to share any of our conspiracy theories with him. So, what did we conclude. Well nothing really. Will we tell the distributors about it back in Auckland, probably not, too much trouble and after all we were in the Islands where things can be 'different.'

The next day.

'Sir do you want it in the bottle or a glass?'
Was the waiter winding us up?

'What do you suggest?'

'No, no sir, your choice.'

'Whatever, a glass will do.'

The beers duly arrive, already poured. We had ordered both Heinekens and Steinlagers. Some serious beer tasting followed, it did not go unnoticed by our waiter. Yep, they're ok, guess yesterday was an aberration, we will never know, however, we did get excellent service from our waiter for the remainder of our stay there.

'Hmmm, better watch it, perhaps not all those holidaymakers from New Zealand are mugs after all.'

Saigon

Vroom, bzzz, toot toot, we're engulfed in a frenzy of mopeds and motor scooters, all tooting away, making a lot of noise as they weave through the traffic. We're passengers on a 'cyclo' in dense Saigon traffic. It's the normal in this crowded city. Every scooter seems to have a fellow driving and a petty girl in a flowing áo dài on the back. We're tourists, and they all call out in English as they flash by. The street is a jungle of traffic, scooters, hundreds of them; mopeds, big old American trucks left over from the war, huge Russian built trucks, dozens of old Citroen cars, relics from French Colonial times. It's an incredible sight.

We had just disembarked from a boat, a French cruise ship; a big high tech yacht. We'd sailed down the coast of Vietnam, and then, a never to be forgotten experience, sailing up the Mekong to Saigon. The river was crowded, hundreds of sampans, fishing boats, and a lot of rusting decrepit looking tramp steamers from Soviet block countries. It was the early nineteen nineties and the war was not long over. We had enjoyed an early breakfast up on deck as we sailed up the river. Vangelis, Conquest of Everest, was on the ships sound system and it created the most incredible atmosphere in this exotic setting; only the French! We have two days here.

The idea was to take in the sights of Saigon, where to start? there's so much. Being on a cyclo in this traffic frenzy was itself an incredible experience. First stop, Ben Thanh market. Never seen anything like it. Everything was for sale in this huge rambling marketplace in the centre of the city, everything. Down at the back, meat and poultry, one look at that! don't go there! the smell! We wandered around the endless alleyways; china, ceramics, fabric, gold, clothes, shoes, metalwork, everything; it was overpowering.

An exotic tea set proved too much; we've used it a lot over the years. The market is under a tin roof and while we were marvelling at what we could buy the heavens opened. The noise from the roof was deafening; perhaps we'll stay awhile.

Outside, eventually. 'One dollar mister.' It's a small boy and he's keen, has everything, biro pens, pocket knives, Vietnamese flags, you name it; 'everything a dollar mister.'

We find our cyclo, he said he would wait, and he did, remarkable. The small boy was persistent running along beside the cyclo, he had several mates, 'one dollar mister, only a dollar.'

Our cyclo takes us on a tour of his city, Ho Chi Minh City, but no one calls it that. I could not help noticing a lot of wall posters warning about aids. The world was engulfed in the aids epidemic at the time and I got the impression it was bad in Vietnam. Another unique thing, kerbside fuel stations. Hundreds of mopeds and scooters need fuel and their needs are catered to by enterprising fellows who dispense petrol from jerry cans at kerbside fuel stations.

There was no let up in the traffic, mopeds, scooters, old Citroens, pretty girls in áo dài's on the back of scooters, calling out to us in English, total bedlam, no let up. There's a big traffic roundabout, Ben Thanh, in the centre of the city and it was absolutely swamped with traffic. The noise was something else, toot, toot, vrumm, vrumm, the occasional screeching of brakes, but no collisions, remarkable, it all worked. Giving way, whose traffic rules, French perhaps,? the French do it differently at roundabouts. Our cyclo is right in there, not a fear in the world, quite normal!

We checked into the Rex Hotel in the centre of Saigon, a remarkable place from the French Colonial period. A huge masonry structure, big rooms, high ceilings, big fans, internal courtyard, very upmarket; well as up market as you can be in a communist country. That evening we went for a walk in the city, a unique experience. The street lighting was poor, the whole place was dark and gloomy and everywhere the propaganda blared out from street loudspeakers, never ending. I had read about this sort of thing, and here it was, it was real. It was the early nineteennineties, the war was not long over. The country was very much under the communist yoke. Straight out of George Orwell's 1984.

'Madam Dai's, you must dine there.'
We had heard this from several sources so off we went in another cyclo, or pedicab as they are sometimes called, it's the way to get around in Saigon. What an experience, La Bibliotheque de Madame Dai is the full name of this famous restaurant. Six rather small tables. We had not booked, did not think about it, we were in luck, they were able to fit us in. There's a big wooden door at the rear of the dining room that opens into the kitchen. Our seat allowed us a good view of this door and every time it opened we were afforded a look into its dark and mysterious interior. Dungeons and dragons and all things spooky came to mind but the food that came through that door was superb, a mixture of French and Vietnamese cuisine.

War Remnants Museum, one of the few places that accepts the Vietnamese dong. Entrance charge 40,000 dong, that's NZ$2.72. Do we want to go there? The word is it's just an exercise in propaganda, 'the war as seen through Vietnamese eyes.' There's the Cu Chi tunnel complex just outside Saigon, and a lot of American war machinery on display as well, but we did not come here to be reminded of war. These days there is a lively café society in Saigon, much more enjoyable. The dong, the Vietnamese currency. Inflation has reduced it to 'confetti money.' The preferred currency is the US$.

Time to leave Saigon. We get a taxi out to Tan Son Nhut airfield.

Inside a car, imagined protection from the traffic mayhem. Arriving at the airport caused us some concern; sure the war is over? Everyone was dressed in military style uniforms, no guns were evident but there was a hostile atmosphere. I had a handycam which I had used a lot, 'evidence of suspicious activity.' I was taken aside and an officious fellow took my camera and proceeded to run right through everything I had recorded. His attitude was a bit of a worry, perhaps I won't be leaving Vietnam today!

Outside the terminal windows a long low wall and behind it dozens, probably hundreds, of American aircraft, all sorts, C130s, Phantoms, helicopters, all left over from the war, rotting away in a huge aircraft graveyard. There was a long line of hardened concrete aircraft revetments all showing obvious damage from the war, now slowly deteriorating, a general air of neglect and decline.

Eventually we made it onto the aircraft that was to take us away from this place. Taxiing out to the runway was another eye opener. The airfield was surrounded by wasteland and jungle and in amongst the vines and undergrowth were dozens of old wrecked aircraft, all sorts, military, and a lot of civilian airliners, Russian Ilyushins, French Caravelles, old DC6's and DC3's, they had all been pushed off the runway into the surrounding jungle and left to rot.

It had been an interesting interlude, perhaps we should have allowed ourselves a bit more time. Another day perhaps.

Hué

Forever associated with the Tet offensive. That bloody conflict cost tens of thousands of lives and marked a turning point in the Vietnam war. Hué, an old Imperial City, was destroyed.

A line of soldiers along the top of the beach, no weapons were evident, but then there was no war, it was over; wasn't it? Do these soldiers know that?

We were landing on this beach, disembarking from the drop down ramp at the front of a small landing craft. Our French cruise ship used this landing craft when there were no docking facilities available. We walked up the steep beach to the line of soldiers. I'm sure the war is over but then this must have been what it used to be like not that long ago and the soldiers would have had guns. Vietnam was opening up to tourism, we were amongst the first wave. It was to be an interesting day.

Bit hard to figure out, the soldiers seemed surly but then after fighting a bloody war against *westerners* I guess it's a bit hard for them to think of us as friends. We made it to the road at the top of the beach and boarded a bus that a tour company had laid on. The drive into the city, what was left of it, was remarkable, not a structure more than one story high, signs of war damage everywhere. Indulge the tourist, it was now government policy, we need their money. It was a modest three story hotel where we were dropped off, the tallest building in the city, the idea was to experience a Vietnamese cultural show and meal. Different, very, and, surprisingly, enjoyable, the hotel staff were trying hard. The show? definitely different, bit slow and monotonous for western ears, very Oriental. The food different, excellent, far removed from anything

I had experienced. The strong French influence was obvious. Then it was up to the roof for a view of Hué. Three stories, nothing else even approached that height. War damage everywhere. Then down to the river for a cruise on the Perfume River, a major waterway that ran past the hotel. Sampans, hundreds of them, the river's a major traffic artery for the city and surrounding area. It was crowded, sampans barely afloat under their heavy loads, everything was transported on the river. Bridges crossed overhead crowded with traffic, opposition tour boats zoomed by, there appeared to be a competitive spirit between the operators. Smaller sampans struggled in the wash of the larger craft. The river banks were crowded with dwellings, all sorts, palatial houses and tumble down shacks, all crowded along the water's edge. After an interesting, very interesting, hour we arrived at an old and famous waterfront Pagoda, Thien Mu. Off the boat and into the crowd, 'one dollar mista,' a cry synonymous with Vietnam, everything 'just a dollar mista.' This time it was coolie hats, had to buy one, still have it. We were besieged by youngsters. White people, I don't think these kids had seen white people in their lives. There was a young French girl with us, blond hair, how can this be? they had to touch it, never seen blond hair. Artworks, beautiful ink drawings, 'two dollar mista,' they were seriously good, had to buy a couple. I'm glad we did, they are a feature on the wall at home, have been for years.

Onto another bus, the historic Imperial Walled City, or what's left of it. The city suffered severely during the Tet offensive. Impressive place and with a little imagination it was not hard to envision what it must have been, war does not allow for history.

The bus again, this time we were to drive down the coast to Da Nang, another place that featured prominently in the war. It took a while to figure out why there were so many small lakes, they were everywhere, the countryside was smothered with these small patches of water; bomb craters, they must have been big bombs. Destroyed bridges were noticeable with new ones built right alongside.

The flat countryside gave way to more mountainous terrain as the road climbed up towards the Hai Van pass where the mountainous part of Vietnam extends out to the coast just north of Da Nang. The Hai Van pass was heavily fortified during the war and the shattered remains of the fortifications were evident everywhere. We stopped and got out of the bus to admire the view. A teenage girl approached us and struck up a conversation, good English. She wanted to go to America, she must have taken us for Americans, the aftermath of war. We continued our drive down into Da Nang where we rejoined our French cruise boat. Noticeable were the grossly overloaded bicycles that appeared to be the main method of transporting goods about the place, huge loads of everything, the bicycle hardly visible beneath it all, different.

Ulm

A beautiful place, on the banks of the Danube in the south of Germany. Tourists love it, clicking away as they pass through on their river cruises. The cathedral, the spire, tallest in the world. Ulm cathedral, or minster, it's not actually a cathedral. Five hundred years to build, the birthplace of Albert Einstein, and a place that very nearly claimed my life. It was that spire, that very tall spire.

Ulm was destroyed by allied bombing in 1944, but the minster, and its spire, survived, curious. A lot of churches, some very famous ones, survived the allied bombing offensive of World War Two, their resident cities totally destroyed yet amongst the carnage a church spire standing tall. Koln Cathedral, or Cologne, is a famous example, why? what explanation can there be?

My encounter with the Ulm spire has been recounted elsewhere, however, I will tell the story again. I was a pilot in NATO's Second Tactical Air Force in Germany. Our squadron was a specialised low flying outfit. We spent all our time thundering around the place at very low level attacking simulated ground targets, fully prepared should the Cold War become a live shooting war, and at the time that was a real possibility; our flying was deadly serious. On this occasion we were given a target in the Donau river valley in Southern Germany. We were required to locate and photograph it to prove that we could indeed have attacked it had it been for real. The time frame to do this was short. The order came down from command and we were required to come up with a result inside a few hours. I was not familiar with the Donau river valley. The weather was poor, low cloud and fog; however, we were practising for war, and war does not just happen on good days. We found ourselves thundering around in unfamiliar territory, low and fast, which was the way we operated, scanning the terrain for this target when suddenly, out of the mist, right in front, there's this spire

Ulm Minster Spire

towering above us, I was not even aware the thing existed. Our planning for this operation was rushed, that's the way these things were done, perhaps a little more study would have revealed the presence of this very tall spire, be aware it's there, please don't knock it down! We missed; the desire to stay alive is very strong. My reaction was instant, however, the heartbeat went off the clock and I had the 'shakes,' bad. My fellow crew member, my navigator, jammed up in the nose of the aeroplane looking forward, the poor fellow must have been terrified by the near miss, the very near miss. It took a little while to recover and eventually we got the required pictures. It was a frightening experience, but we were practising for war, and war can be fatal.

I've often thought about that incident, we could have been killed and the world would have remembered us as the irresponsible people who destroyed the Ulm Minster's spire, the tallest in the world, the one that took five hundred years to build and seconds to destroy, but it did not happen, close though!

A Moment In History

Saturday night, August 12th 1961, the world changed. The Berlin Wall. I was there. It happened at midnight; I will never forget it.

That morning I had been in East Berlin, crossed at the Brandenburg gate, probably one of the last people from the west to do so. Now the Brandenburg Gate was sealed off with an ugly barbed wire entanglement preventing all access. It stayed like that for the next twenty-eight years.

How come I was there for that moment in history, a lad from the other side of the earth, deep inside the Soviet Bloc. Great moments in history are seldom signalled, they just happen. I was doing the *'rite of passage'* thing that youngsters from the antipodes did at that time, *the big OE.* Mine lasted eight years and took me all over the world. One of the places I just happened to be was Berlin on August 12th and 13th 1961. It was rugby that put me there on that fateful weekend.

I was in the RAF in Germany, part of the West's military response to the threat posed by the Warsaw Pact. Being from New Zealand it was assumed I would be a good rugby player, wrong, I was an ordinary rugby player, but keen. The British Military in Germany fielded numerous rugby teams and a big attraction was playing the Gatow team. Gatow was an airfield in Berlin that gave the British a token presence in the divided city. Playing Gatow meant a weekend in Berlin.

We played on the Saturday afternoon in the old Olympic Stadium, Hitler's 1936 showpiece. It survived the war intact, an impressive place. You may have seen it in old newsreels. Hitler used it for numerous rallies in the period leading up to World War Two. That rugby game was a turning point in my life, the last game I ever played. Carried off in the second half with four cracked ribs, that's it, I'm over rugby. I was patched up and able to enjoy Saturday night out in the city with my mates, albeit a bit constrained. Berlin had superb pubs and beer cellars. There was tension in the air, an uneasy feeling, I think the locals noticed it more than us. I recall getting to bed sometime after midnight, the next morning, *the world had changed.*

August 13th 1961

During the early hours of Sunday the East Germans had erected a barbed wire barrier right across the western side of the Brandenburg Gate, the start of *the wall.* It would be twenty-eight years, 1989, before it was dismantled.

We went along to have a look, an ugly mess of barbed wire blocking all access to the east. It was the previous morning that I, and a couple of others, had been through the Brandenburg Gate into East Berlin. The gate is just on the eastern side of the border and was a recognised crossing point. One of the attractions of going into East Berlin was simply, that you could do it. We thought that was pretty cool. There was a Polish Culture shop that sold very cheap records, Supraphon, classical only, no decadent western pop. Plenty of bus tours on offer, the sights of East Berlin. The only sights were huge communist style monuments and statues to the heroic Soviet liberators of 1945. Propaganda was 'in your face' at every turn, pretty dreary place. These things happened at the height of the Cold War. It never ceased to amaze me that I was allowed into East Berlin. I was a pilot on a NATO nuclear strike squadron. I had valuable targeting information in my head. What if the STASI had picked me off the street? but they never did. Was it a high stakes game being played out or was it sheer incompetence. I will never know, but then I was very young and those thoughts never entered my head.

I've followed the wall's history over the years, the sheer horror of the thing. East Germany became a huge prison, no escape, probably death if you tried.

I was witness to its creation on that fateful weekend in Berlin, a moment in history.

Istanbul Two

AAaaHHaaEEeeaahhAAaa, right in my ear, *and loud*. Suddenly I'm wide-awake, what the devil? It's six in the morning, the Islamic call to prayer. We're in a Muslim country, remember. There's a mosque just across the cobbled street outside the window that's down at street level, right by the head of our bed. What's made it worse, we had opened the window a little after the traffic noise had died down the previous evening. No more sleep for us, close the window quick. Early rising could be a feature of our Istanbul experience. It's our second day in Istanbul, the events of day one have been recounted in an earlier story, what's on the program today?

Our good tour organiser has done a brilliant job so far, free lunch for her anytime, let's see how today goes. First up, the Blue Mosque, a must see. Breakfast in the hotel's little dining room. It's ok; just, very Mediterranean, nothing to get your teeth into, not my thing. The others reckon I'm being difficult, I think they have convinced themselves that it must be good because we are in an exotic place; maybe? but it does not satisfy me. We come from New Zealand, expectations are high. At home we enjoy very good food, something I don't think we appreciate, take it for granted. The rest of the world does not necessarily enjoy quite the same standard. When we go abroad we have to accept this. Let's not dwell on it, we eat too much anyway. What about those kerbside kebabs yesterday? Döner kebabs, they were right up there, nothing like that in New Zealand.

Breakfast over, out onto the street. We'll walk, everything a tourist wants to see is within walking distance, the Arena Hotel, good choice. Off we go, more fascinating street scenes, more pictures, we have a lot of pictures. A short walk and we're there, the Blue Mosque, and a zillion people. We join a line, a very long line, it appears to be moving right along. In no time at all we are doing the shoes in hand thing and we're in. Standing in that line was a unique experience, the people, every nationally you could imagine, the languages, the way they dressed, the sheer variety of it all, bit different to New Zealand. Inside, what a sight, the place is huge, the top of the dome way up there in the stratosphere. The colours, the intricate decoration, just incredible, more pictures, bit challenging this time, the light is difficult. There's a blue tinge to everything. We spend some time shuffling through the place, it's big. The crush of people determined just how fast you progressed. I was impressed, again. Spending a lot of time being impressed in Istanbul, unlike anything I have ever seen. Another place for your bucket list. There were numerous domes, all big, each one included unique windows and colourful tile work. All this dome watching required a lot of 'head up.' The predominate colour 'up above' was blue and this gave a blue tinge to everything.

Outside, eventually, shoes on and we wander along Sultanahmet Square, it's dominated by the Hagia Sophia. Sultanahmet Square is an experience in itself, extraordinary sights, colourful people, all unique to this fabulous city. Hagia Sophia, it's huge, dates back to the sixth century. How did they build such incredible edifices so long ago. It's been a Christian Church, a mosque and a museum and it's full of old icons, sculptures, and relics of all sorts. We spent several hours inside marvelling at it all, then outside into the bright sunlight, bit gloomy in there. Down to the Topkapi Palace near the waterfront, another spectacular sight, the centre of the Ottoman court for over four hundred years. Everywhere in this city we are aware of how much history surrounds us, the country cousins from New Zealand.

The Topkapi Palace, it's huge, one of the biggest palaces in the world Dozens of architectural marvels spread over a huge area. A harem that used to house hundreds of wives and concubines, an enormous kitchen building, a huge armoury. All the structures are incredibly ornate, works of art really, nothing like it anywhere else in the world. The whole place reflected the wealth and power of the Ottoman dynasty who named the place Constantinople when they defeated the Romans in the fifteenth century and converted the place to Islam. They lasted for five hundred years until the end of World War one. The Ottomans aligned themselves with the losing side. Pfiff, gone in a flash. Constantinople was renamed Istanbul in nineteen-thirty, a more 'Turkish' sounding name

We found ourselves in a crush of people. The Topkapi Palace is an incredibly popular tourist attraction and we were tourists ticking off our bucket list items. There it was in a glass cabinet. A big fellow, with an even bigger gun, right there as well. The Topkapi diamond, one of the biggest in the world.

Istanbul, the most populous city in the world, sixteen million people live there, thirty-eight universities, three thousand mosques. It's located at the junction of the Bosphorus and the Golden Horn and commands a spectacular view of both. It's the most visited city in the world, twenty million people each year.

A trip on the Bosphorus, the waterway that divides Europe and Asia, another 'must do.' There's a well organised four-hour boat trip that takes in all the sights, and there are some spectacular sights. A little yellow cab, there are a lot of little yellow cabs in Istanbul. Down to the waterfront and a big ferry with lots of seating on an open deck. Off we go towards the Black Sea end, and Russia, hugging the western shoreline, the European side. All along the water's edge there are mosques, forts, palaces, hotels, and big mansions. They've been there a long time, very ornate, reflecting their Ottoman origins. These structures are amongst the world's most expensive real estate, many are Russian owned. There's a big Russian presence. It's in their interest to be here. The Bosphorus, is the only warm water access Russia has to the world.

The bridges to Asia, three of them across the Bosphorus and a fourth across the Dardanelles just to the south, enormous structures, amongst the biggest suspension bridges in the world. There's a two-level tunnel as well at the southern end of the Bosphorus, the Avrasya tunnel, one of the engineering marvels of the world.

The Turks are responsible for some of the biggest most ambitious engineering feats of modern times. The Avrasya, or its more usual name, the Eurasia tunnel, is the most ambitious tunnelling project ever undertaken anywhere and the bridges are amongst the world's greatest structures. The Canakkali Bridge that spans the Dardanelles is the longest suspension bridge in the world.

We pass under the Fatih Sultan Mehmet bridge, it towers above us, a hundred and seventy metres above us, hard to comprehend the size of it.

Very busy place the Bosphorus, all sorts of shipping use this strategic waterway. It's the only shipping access for the Balkan states, Bulgaria, Romania, Moldova, the Ukraine, Crimea, and Russia, they're all dependant on it. All this shipping, huge tankers to small fishing vessels, and our sightseeing boat skilfully avoiding all the traffic. We marvel at the places crowding the water's edge, a lot of wealth here. Private mansions, mostly Russian owned, they're small palaces, and the pleasure boats, huge yachts, there are a lot of them. We reach the northern end of our tour, turn back, and travel down the eastern shore, the Asian or Anatolian side, what a contrast. Gone are the lofty Ottoman stone structures, the forts and palaces, everything is wood, big ornate wooden mansions and not so many luxurious pleasure yachts. The tour is a real experience for us, unlike anything I have ever seen.

Back at the ferry terminal we elect to walk to our hotel, walking in Istanbul is so fascinating. Not long to opening time and we can have a beer in this Muslim country.

Dinner, and in Istanbul we're spoilt for choice. The place to go is Istiklal Street, a huge selection of eating places from streetside vendors to full restaurants. Another little yellow cab and we're there, atmosphere to burn. We pick a likely looking outdoor restaurant, seat ourselves, order some wine, then tackle the menu, different! Not a problem. An English-speaking waiter is very helpful, in no time he's sorted us out, don't know what the dishes are but it's all good. One thing that did impress me was lavash, puff, or balloon bread, a big puffball of delicious dough, put it on your bucket list. We ate well, the Turks enjoy good food, then another little yellow cab, home to bed, and try and get some sleep before that 'call to prayer' from across the street.

Day three, our last day, we got that wrong, need more than three days; next time perhaps? We decide on a sightseeing tour, they are good, stress-free as well. Along the length of the Golden Horn, a stretch of water that divides Istanbul into a northeast and a southwest part. There are several bridges, nowhere near those that span the Bosphorus. The Golden horn bridges are much smaller lower structures, too low for ships, but then there's not much shipping on the Golden horn. What is noticeable are the people fishing. Some of the bridges are packed with men hanging rods out over the water, the Galata Bridge is particularly popular. It's more of a social thing with the men but they do catch fish, small fellows, anchovies, mullet, small albacore and Bonito. Across on the northern side the skyline is dominated by the very old historic Galata Tower. We get off our bus and walk around Balat, an old part of the city notable for its brightly coloured two storied wooden houses. There are a lot of parks and woodland around the upper reaches of the Golden Horn, it's a peaceful and relaxing part of Istanbul.

Our tour bus drops us off in Sultanahmet Square, not far from our hotel. It's our last day, a long flight back to New Zealand that night, not looking forward to it; how about another good meal. The Sultanahmet part of the city is home to a lot of excellent restaurants and we settle for one that looks good with an attractive sidewalk eating area. We get lucky, it's really good. The waiters help with the menu and we order up big, could be a while before the next decent meal. I go for the lavash again, something I had discovered earlier, great 'balloons' of puff bread, delicious, I'm a bread nut and this lavsh was right up there.

We linger over the meal in the late afternoon sunshine, Istanbul has been a highlight for us. I want to go back, need more time, a lot more time, however, right now, it's the big aeroplane, and a long, long flight.

The Lagoon

They crashed up against the coral reef, huge landing craft, the ramps dropped and enormous machines rumbled down into the shallow water on the inside of the reef. The biggest earth moving monsters' American industry could produce. They crashed their way across the shallow lagoon, up the beach and immediately went to work flattening a large area of what was already a level piece of terrain. The operation had been well planned. Create a landing strip big enough to take a B29 bomber, and do it just as fast as you can. The explosion of activity continued non-stop for forty-eight hours, and it was done. PSP metal mesh was laid and the first B29 landed twelve hours later. The supply ships were standing offshore with fuel and bombs. It was all brought across the reef onto the new crushed coral airfield and loaded into the B29s. They took off immediately and bombed the next Japanese occupied island, surprise was total. Where had these bombers come from? The Pacific, nineteen forty-three, America's massive response to Japanese expansionism.

We flew up to the islands across the beautiful blue Pacific, to this place in paradise, an exotic coral island resort. The aircraft landed on the old wartime airstrip, the PSP still up to it after all these years, the island's lifeline to the outside world, without it they would be isolated. The attraction, the scuba diving, this place was right up with the world's best. The big lagoon was incredibly interesting, one of the few places on the planet that benefitted from the brutality of war.

We waded out into the lagoon near the airfield, no more than knee deep in most places, coral outcrops everywhere, the fish life incredible, and in amongst it all these big outcrops covered in marine growth projecting up above the water, they were metal, very old metal, the remains of those huge earthmoving machines the Americans had brought ashore all those years ago. Huge engine blocks, all that was left of those monster machines, axial differentials, gearboxes, enormous, how big were those machines? It was quite sobering to realize that right here was where the Pacific war was fought, a brutal conflict costing hundreds of thousands of lives, little quarter was given, there were few prisoners. The detritus of war was everywhere when you went looking, and you had to really look, the jungle had reclaimed everything. The most obvious left overs were the remains of those huge earthmoving machines, they were not going easily those big pieces of engine, they would feature in the lagoon for years to come. The airfield, a bonus of war, without it this place would be an unknown backwater accessible only by boat, and that would be difficult, there's no natural harbour.

We spent a lot of time exploring the lagoon, a tranquil place now. What was it like all those years ago when the world was at war, countries fighting each other, unable to get along, expansionism, blind determination to rule the world, man's unstoppable desire to subjugate his fellow man. There were no rules, well there were but some countries ignored them and this made the conflict vicious, unforgiving, no quarter given. In this idyllic place death and destruction was an everyday occurrence. Now there are these slowly corroding metal monuments to man's inability to get along with his fellows, a sobering realisation when you get to thinking about how these things came to be here. The war is long gone, all those people involved are also gone. There are very few veterans remaining from '*the world at war*.' Nature has taken over, turned the detritus of war to its advantage. The wreckage in the lagoon has been colonised by nature. When you don mask and snorkel a wondrous world opens up. Myriads of colourful little fish live amongst all this, it's their home. If man had not provided what would these little fellows do? where would they live? War was a good thing for nature in this place.

The creation of the airfield changed the whole ecosystem in the lagoon, possibly for the better, provided more habitat, more hidey-holes. As we puddled around awed by it all, numerous small creatures appeared, popped out of their hiding places to have a look at us, these big creatures invading their domain. It was their predecessors who created this, our habitat, but we don't know that, we spend our days ducking in and out of all these little spaces, mostly corral but a lot of them are some other much harder stuff, mans' contribution.

The diving happened outside the lagoon over the reef in deep water, and it could be very deep. Sliding down the gently sloping wall of corral was an incredible experience. Be careful, too easy to become absorbed by the beauty of the place, fascinated by the life existing in the corral, inattention to depth could suddenly culminate in the realization that you are too deep, the wall of corral just kept on going down. It was home to a lot of painted crayfish, inaccessible, way back in their holes but they were vulnerable at certain times, the locals had it figured. When the moon, tide, and time of month all came together in a particular combination the crays come up from the depths in the evening, over the reef into the shallow lagoon and wander around for several hours, then back over the reef and down to the depths. The locals wade around in the shallows and pick them up, easy-peasy.

'Coca Cola bottle mister, one dollar.' The kids were selling coke bottles from yesteryear, the old original waisted heavy glass ones from the nineteen forties. The Americans brought in hundreds of thousands of them, the empties were buried, along with a lot of other stuff in big pits. The island kids dug up the pits and sold the bottles, not a silly idea, they were collector's items. The war left mountains of 'stuff' behind. Huge quantities of war material had been brought in, everything from coke bottles to those huge earth moving machines, aircraft, trucks, an incredible amount of 'stuff,' and suddenly the war ends. There's all this stuff lying around, what do we do with it, can't take it home, uneconomic. Sell the big stuff to the local administration, the heavy machines will be very useful to the local Government however we are not Father Christmas, there will be a token charge for these things, trucks, earth moving machines. What? no? won't pay? reckon it'll be left here anyway, we'll get it for nix? Wrong, very wrong, you're being greedy, we're offering it at ridiculously low prices, but it's not for free, you will have to pay something, that's fair. 'No, we won't pay, we'll call your bluff.'

The locals were not good poker players and taking on the Americans was a no brainer. 'If you don't want to pay something for it, we'll just destroy it.' 'No you won't, your bluffing,' not bluffing. The Americans pushed everything out over the reef into deep water that's how those big bits got to be in the lagoon, got stuck, everything else went over the reef. Some 'stuff' did survive. There were a few beat up trucks still running around, and a lot of coca cola bottles.

We spent two weeks on the island, it was paradise, far removed from the nineteen forties, from war and destruction, a peaceful place. There were few signs of war remaining, nature had reclaimed what it had previously owned, the jungle had swallowed everything, completely covered the mess that man had left, restored the place's natural beauty, a place of peace and quiet again.

'Coke bottle mister, one dollar.'
And those huge chunks of iron out in the lagoon.

The Yacht Moored Outside

It's white, moored in the estuary outside our big view window the early morning sun lighting it up, and the shoreline beyond, a striking sight. It's identical to another setting, a white yacht moored outside a hotel room in Tahiti under a palm tree, the main reef in the background, early morning sun lighting it up. Both scenes almost the same, the timing, years apart. The yacht in the estuary is now, Tahiti yacht, yesteryear, but time is of no consequence, both scenes are timeless. Estuary yacht I see every morning, Tahiti yacht, a memory.

It's not always a pleasant sunny scene, the weather can be foul sometimes, the estuary thrashed by big waves and gale force winds. Estuary yacht straining on its mooring, trying to break free and crash onto the beach. Tahiti yacht suffered tropical cyclones occasionally, its mooring being severally tested. There was the time when the mooring was not up to it. Tahiti yacht broke free and smashed onto the beach, a gaping hole in its side. The next time I saw Tahiti yacht it was back at its place outside the hotel like nothing had happened.

I travelled to Tahiti countless times, always *the Captain's room*. Tahiti yacht is forever fixed in my memory. These days my travelling is finished. I live in a cottage on a beach, estuary yacht right outside. On the good days I gaze out at estuary yacht and reminisce, it's wonderful.

Under The Rialto

Two tall Peroni glasses frosted with condensation, complimentary pizza. A Japanese wedding party struggling with a photo shoot out on a pontoon amidst all the bustling gawking tourists. Gondoliers plying their wares, water taxis buzzing around, and it's noisy. We are in a small open-air cafe under the Rialto Bridge enjoying a beer, an incredible atmosphere, straight Hollywood.

We've left the girls to do their thing, shop till you drop, not our scene. Soaking up the atmosphere, the sounds, the sights, the hustle and bustle, infinitely more enjoyable. It's landed us in this café, right up there on the bucket list. We are soaking it up, the Venetian experience. Our little table commanded a view of the activity. it seemed the whole world was right here, all these people, a microcosm of the world, where else, another beer, I don't want to leave this spot, it's unique, nowhere else in the world.

We had flown in from Athens that morning, a day in Venice, then we sail out from the centre of the city on a big cruise ship, right along the main canal, right past the thousands of tourists, the famous buildings, out into the Adriatic, a truly memorable experience.

I want to go back, do it all again, another trip to Europe. The Rialto thing summed it all up. The complete Venetian immersion experience. Ripped off? yes, expected, but it was done so nicely.

A full on day, arrive in the morning, sail out that evening. Did the water taxi thing, the glass blowing on Murano, should have bought that dancing horse the fellow made before my very eyes. The brightly painted houses on Burano, the masks, the leaning towers. The Venetians of yesteryear were not very good at foundations.

We walked and walked, along the canal, the Doge's Palace, the crowds of tourists, St Mark's square, the Basilica, the Bridge of Sighs, all the famous places, and it was great. When we were completely 'touristed' out we boarded the big boat, the cruise liner that was going to take us around the eastern Mediterranean to Istanbul, it had been a full on day.

Venice, I want to go back.

Eating Places

On my journey through life I've enjoyed eating at some interesting places around the world. Some of them you would not call restaurants in the accepted sense of the word, definitely not. Places where the food is the thing, not the surroundings. Places with character, places that might upset a discerning diner who's looking for a certain standard. The places I'm going to tell you about fall well short of these expectations. The food's the thing, well in my mind it is. If the food is good other considerations don't matter so much.

Fatty's – Singapore

In the 1960s, early 70s, Fatty's was an institution in Singapore. Located in Albert Street, it was popular with airline crew from all over the world, a great meeting place. Unfortunately the original Fatty's is no more. There are modern versions operating under the same name but they are far removed from the uniqueness of the original Albert Street Fatty's. It was part of a house-shop, a unique structure found all over Singapore at that time. A two-storey building with a shop or business on the ground floor and living quarters above. These house-shops were all joined together and formed a wall along each side of the street. Fatty's had been modified. The front of the place opened out onto the street, there was no front wall, and the ground floor ceiling had gone which made the inside very spacious. There was a mezzanine where the upper level had been and a stairway accessed a toilet up on the mezzanine. Diners were accommodated at large round tables that came in several sizes. When the inside was full the tables spilled out onto the street and that was nearly all the time. It was not the cleanest of places, in fact it was not a place for the squeamish, but after a few beers, which was always the case, who cares. The food was good, basically Chinese with a few of Fatty's specials thrown in. The owner, Fatty of course, a jovial rotund fellow of Chinese extraction, was usually present keeping an eye on things. I ate there frequently. There was a downside, the mezzanine toilet, not for the faint hearted. A hole in the floor affair, no seat, and rather unsanitary surroundings, common in the Orient at the time; but as I've said, the food was excellent.

Café de Kerb – Limassol

When I lived in Germany flying for NATO's Second Tactical Air Force we were frequent visitors to Cyprus. Akrotiri, a big British base on the south coast of the Island was a place where we did a lot of air to ground gunnery and dive bombing. There was this 'café de kerb' in the local town, Limassol, a popular place late at night when the beer was talking and we were hungry. Kebabs with plenty of peanut sauce was the thing. The idea was to tell the vendor, a hard case Cypriot fellow, what you wanted and he would prepare it all on a charcoal BBQ right there on the side of the road. The routine was to sit on the kerb and drink more beer while the 'chef' did his thing. There were several RAF strike squadrons based at Akrotiri and we knew some of the pilots. They were always keen to take us to their 'favourite restaurant.' The service was excellent and the kebabs delicious. I never had any problems eating there but I think the tummy was well fortified with all the beer.

Cold Storage – Singapore

A place I became familiar with in my airline days. Down Orchard road to Cold Storage, a big supermarket. Across the road from the supermarket was a carpark that accommodated several hawker food stalls in the evening; it was good. The downside, a large open drain along one side of the carpark, but that did not matter, the food was good, and the food was what we were after. Again, this tended to be a place we visited later in the evening after a lot of beer at the Tanglin Inn, our favourite pub. Kebabs was what they did at Cold Storage and they came with a lot of peanut sauce. They were good and it was tempting to over eat but caution was required. There was a lot of peanut sauce and it was easy to over indulge. An excess of peanut oil can cause problems as I found out one night. A group of us had been in our favourite pub, the Tanglin Inn, an old and famous establishment in Tanglin Road, and over several hours, as well as drinking a lot of beer, we consumed a lot of peanuts. The barman kept filling up the peanut bowl and we, or perhaps I should say I, kept eating them, I love peanuts. Nothing wrong with that, however, later in the evening it was down to Cold Storage and into the kebabs with lashings of peanut sauce, in my case a lot of peanut sauce. Great meal, back to our hotel, into bed.

Three in the morning, oh dear, I am seriously crook, and vomiting. It turned out to be peanut oil poisoning, something that's not easy to do, however, I had managed it, not nice. Can't blame the dubious location of the hawker stalls. Others in the group did not have a problem, just me, and my over indulgence in peanuts. It lasted for forty-eight hours and I would not wish it upon anyone.

Banana Leaf Apolo

An Indian restaurant. Another experience from my airline days, very basic. You needed a strong constitution to eat there. I liked the place, the food was excellent, but I cannot say the same about the surroundings. I guess you could not call it a favourite place to eat apart from a small group of us, I was one of them. These days I believe there's a restaurant with the same name in Singapore that's quite upmarket, definitely not the place I knew when I was a regular visitor to that city. My Banana Leaf Apollo was way down market, but the food was great. It was in a scruffy part of town and the appearance of the place? well it looked like a slum. Inside it was dark and scungy, the furniture was rough, and there were no eating utensils. You went in, sat down, and a fellow came around and slapped a large section of banana leaf on the table, shortly after that another fellow came along with a big open kerosene can full of food, he scooped out a handful and slapped it on the banana leaf.

'Enough? another handful perhaps?'

That was it, you ate with your fingers. It was an endless meal, if you wanted more, then another handful was readily available, no extra charge. It was a curry, not sure what was in there but it was always good, well I thought so. As you ate, make sure your shirtsleeves are rolled up, a yellow stain seemed to creep slowly up your arms, if it came into contact with your clothing then I am not sure you would ever get it out. Large bottles of Tiger beer were available, the old-style big bottle. Every time you handled the bottle a yellow lumpy deposit from your hands would adhere to it. After a while the bottle looked disgusting. You are probably thinking, what were you doing going to such a dump, well the food was really good and talk about character, this place had heaps. There were a couple of drawbacks. Occasionally, when we had sweet talked the girls into coming out with us for dinner at *an authentic Indian restaurant* there would be a rebellion when we fronted this particular one.

'I'm not going in there!' and that would be the end of it.
Another downer, and I must agree, this one really was bad, the toilet, do not go to the toilet, a hole in the floor, filthy, no toilet paper. But to repeat myself, the food was great, and so much character!

Ben Thanh Market – Saigon

No longer Saigon, it's now Ho Chi Minh City. Ben Thanh covered market in the centre of the city is huge. A fascinating place where everything is for sale, definitely a *bucket list* thing. At the rear of the market there's a food hall, different! You can smell it as you work your way towards the rear of the place. The food area is dominated by what we would call an abattoir. All sorts of creatures are slaughtered and prepared for human consumption in this area, it's stomach turning, and the smell! There are food stalls there, but would you? I couldn't. If you ever find yourself in this market go to the back and have a look; a once in a lifetime experience.

The 'Black Hole' - Hong Kong

There was one place in Hong Kong that defied description, an eating establishment that was unbelievably horrible. Let me attempt to describe it. A place for the Chinese labourers who worked on the many construction sites in the area. A large rambling single storey wooden structure that had seen better years; it was practically falling down. There were no lights inside, the interior was dark and intimidating with many years of filth on everything. Outside on the street people were squatting on the pavement preparing food in the gutter and using the water from the gutter to do it. Unbelievable but true, the smell was stomach turning. Inside there were customers actually eating which never ceased to amaze me. Walking past this place was an ordeal, it actually made me feel sick. It was not necessary to walk past, you could cross to the other side of the street but we didn't, a sort of morbid fascination with the place. As I recall it occupied a corner at the bottom of Ashley Road. I'm sure it's long gone but it's right there in my memory, how could you ever forget it, the stuff of nightmares.

Narita Village – Japan

During my airline years I stayed in a hotel in Narita village, just outside Tokyo, many times, and frequented numerous restaurants there. They were a mixed bag, all very Japanese and mostly catering to Japanese tastes. The 'goings on' inside some of these was stomach turning, and the smells! You would have to be a brave westerner with an adventurous spirit to venture inside some of these places. I was not that adventurous! We did eat at several that catered specifically to airline crew. The waiters spoke English, and they knew the sorts of things that would appeal. I enjoyed numerous good meals in Narita restaurants.

Minwalla's - Ismaili Karachi

A real dump. My experience of the place was in the nineteen fifties. I don't think the particular Minwalla's I experienced still exists; a good thing too, the place was bad news. I was in the Air Force and we used to pass through the place frequently. Minwalla's at Ismaili was where we were accommodated and, unfortunately, also the place where we were required to eat. It was a disaster every time, dysentery, unavoidable. I even resorted to not eating anything during our short stop overs, did not even clean my teeth, still suffered dysentery, must be in the air.

There was one compensation, camel riding on the local beach. Not many places where you can experience that, but zip your lip, let nothing pass. Didn't work, the trots every time we went near the place.

There were other suspect places I encountered in my travels. I found I developed a 'sense' for these, the odd mistake but generally my experience was that there was good eating at some unlikely places. I should mention Bali. There are street vendors everywhere, particularly at Kuta Beach, but caution is required, they are not all good, a lot of dodgy ones, however, some of the small charcoal kebab vendors are ok.

There is another factor that needs to be considered if you want to eat *offline*, alcohol. To put it crudely, a skinful of beer definitely helps to ward off tummy bugs.

You're Under Arrest Sir

'Excuse me?'

'You're under arrest sir.'

Excuse me indeed, how can this be?

I was at the immigration desk at Los Angeles airport, just got off a big jet after flying all the way from Auckland, when I was confronted with this. *I was the Captain.*

'There's an outstanding arrest warrant for you sir.'

'Can't be, there's some mistake.'

'No mistake sir, the warrant was issued two months ago, got your name on it.'

'But I've not been in America for three months, what crime am I guilty of?'

'An unpaid parking ticket sir.'

There was the trace of a smile on the immigration man's face.

'Looks like you failed to pay a parking infringement some time ago, not a good idea in California sir.'

'Ok, I think I can see what's happened. Are you going to handcuff me now in front of my crew and cart me off to jail?'

'No, I'll spare you that, I'll allow you twenty-four hours to sort it out; *but,* you must sort it or it will be the handcuffs.'

The fellow's smiling now, seen it all before. The rest of the crew are not party to this conversation, except the Flight Engineer, he's grinning.

'In the shit Captain, can we visit you in jail?'

The immigration fellow tells me I can call at any Police Station. I'm in the computer system so the problem can be sorted at any of them, *but,* I must do it now, time has run out for this heinous offense. So what had happened, how had I transgressed?

At the time the airline had several crews based in Los Angeles to operate their Los Angeles to London service. Doing it this way allowed better utilisation of crew. It was a popular move. Live in Los Angeles for three months, an apartment on Venice Beach, all expenses paid, life was complete. I had done two of these and they were as good as advertised, however, there was one problem, transport, you really need a car to get the most out of living in Southern California. There was so much to see and do and public transport did not cut the mustard.

When I first moved into an apartment at Venice beach I purchased a car, a second hand Ford Granada, a long low two door freeway flyer, a real Detroit special, perfect for Southern California. I drove all over the state, into Nevada, clocked up thousands of miles, had a great time, however, I had to come back to Auckland at the end of the three months. I will be doing that again, I had decided. What do I do with the car? Everyone who did one of these three month stints needed transport so I took to leasing it out to other pilots and engineers. This worked well, there was plenty of demand; and the source of my run in with the law.

The wife of a fellow who had leased the car had incurred a parking ticket. Like a good Auckland motorist she just ignored it; doesn't work like that in California. If a parking fine is not settled by the due date the fine is doubled. If it continues to go unpaid then it's doubled again. This process goes on for some time, the fine getting bigger rapidly. There is a limit. Eventually an unpaid ticket triggers an arrest warrant for the vehicle owner, in this case, me.

We were staying in a hotel in Westwood at the time and I went along to the local Police station to *sort it out*. At that stage I only knew what the immigration fellow had told me at the airport. The fellow I dealt with at the Police station was friendly and helpful, and rather amused. Perusal of the computer records revealed the time and place of the original ticket and I was able to put a name to who had leased the car at that time. The upshot of this, I was allowed one week for the outstanding fine to be paid. It was up around five hundred dollars by now. I did not inquire what would happen if the fine was not paid inside a week. I think I had used up all the leniency the police were going to allow.

I was back in Auckland three days later and gave my fellow pilot a call. He was not aware of the ticket; understandable. I made it very clear that payment was required *now* and gave him the relevant bank and police reference numbers.

I don't want to think about the possible *domestic* my call might have triggered.

I was rostered for Los Angeles again in two weeks-time. I had not heard back from my errant pilot friend so I was a bit tensed up when I fronted immigration.

'Welcome to America sir, enjoy your stay.'

If New Zealand had a system like California for collecting outstanding fines then the jails would be overflowing. They do things differently in California.

Murphy's

'It'll be a Murphy's sonny.'
'Excuse me?'
'Murphy's, that's what we drink 'round here.'

I was in a bar in Cork, fresh off the plane from New Zealand. Ireland, first time, and I had committed a capital crime, asking for a Guinness in Southern Ireland.

'Ah yes, of course, a Murphy's'
'That's better laddie; from New Zealand?'

The barman was a character. He'd picked me straight away and decided to have a bit of fun at my expense. Sonny, laddie, and me all of seventy years. My first lesson in things Irish and I'm glad it happened. Murphy's, a delightful drop, leaves Guinness for dead. I was introduced to something I did not even know existed; love at first taste.

This little incident set the tone for our visit to Southern Ireland. We spent a week there, Murphy's at all the pubs, not a Guinness in sight.

There was a similar incident many years ago in Australia. We had driven up from Sydney into Queensland, crossed the NSW border, adjusted our watches, they're different in Queensland, and stopped at the first town we came to, the intention being to stay the night. The hotel was a big rambling two story wooden affair from yesteryear, bat wing doors, real outback. Big garden bar, middies and schooners, all very Australian. Living in Sydney I had become rather partial to Reschs beer, reaching Reschs we called it. I fronted the bar and asked for a Reschs; capital crime in Queensland. The rather large barman leaned over, clenched fists on his bar, and informed me it would be a Forex or Blimba, 'no namby pamby New South Wales rubbish here *laddie!*' What he meant, I could have a Four xxxx or a Bulimba beer, the two local Queensland brews, very parochial in Queensland.

'Of course, silly me, make it two Four xxxx please.'

'That's better *laddie.*'

The barman turned out to be a character, he had picked us as Kiwis and decided to take the piss, 'can't let an opportunity like that slip by.'

The Mekong

One of the world's great rivers. Rising in the plateaus of Tibet it flows for 3000 miles, 5000 kilometres, through South East Asia emptying into the South China Sea near Saigon. Years ago, I enjoyed an unforgettable experience sailing up the Mekong from the South China Sea to Saigon, Ho Chi Minh City these days. It was on a big five masted high tech French yacht owned by the Club Mediterranée, a once in a lifetime experience.

We had sailed down the Vietnamese coast, calling at Halong Bay, Hué, Da Nang, Phú Luong, Nha Trang, all these places were an incredible experience, then early one morning, up the lower reaches of the mighty Mekong to Saigon. It was a French boat and the war was not long over. I think the French were 'testing the waters.' The previous day, before entering the Mekong, the Vietnamese authorities came aboard and took an extraordinary amount of time examining every passport on the ship, about four hundred, it went on for most of the day. Perhaps the French were not prepared to come up with the necessary bribe, who knows. Not long after this the French discontinued the Club Med's 'Vietnam experience' which was a pity, it was something quite unique.

The Mekong, it's a mighty river and this big yacht was getting along at quite a clip, Vangelis's Conquest of Paradise blaring out on the sound system, it seemed so appropriate, very impressive. There was a lot of shipping on the river, hundreds of small fishing boats, all shapes and sizes, a lot of old rusty Eastern European freight ships, equally decrepit Russian freighters, bulk carriers, all sorts. What was noticeable, no western flagged ships. We're in a communist country, it screamed at us from all directions; an unforgettable experience.

I was particularly interested in what we were looking at. It was not long after the war, something I've read about a lot. Jungle lined both sides of the river, came right down into the water, no visible land and there were a lot of small waterways running into the main river. During the war the Viet Cong owned the river. They had a lot of gun positions hidden right down in the jungle at the water's edge, a real danger for any shipping on the river.

While we were glued to the ships railing taking it all in, well it was just such an extraordinary sight, others were not. Nearly everyone on the ship was French and they were pretty laid back. There was a fitness class for the girls out by the pool, a lot of people asleep in the sun loungers, people in the numerous bars, and us, gawking at the sights. The whole thing was surreal, something I will never forget. It continued on for several hours until we reached the port part of the river, Saigon, where we tied up at a broken-down floating berth, not the greatest, but we were from the west, not going to get anything special here.

We enjoyed an excellent late breakfast and then it was the sights of Saigon, Ho Chi Minh City.

About The Author

After a lifetime of flying, both military and civil, Rex Mangin now lives in a cottage on a beach in Auckland New Zealand. There are a lot of memories. They are worth sharing and this collection of short stories attempts to do that.

Books By Rex Mangin

These books by Rex Mangin are available as paperbacks, and at all e-book outlets worldwide, or you can contact the author at: rex.mangin@xtra.co.nz.

Infidelity Gun Running
&
Other Tales

Fourteen short stories drawn from the author's vast treasure trove of experiences. He spent a lifetime in aviation, both military and civilian, became involved in the Cold War in Europe, nuclear testing at Christmas Island, topdressing in New Zealand, and spent many years flying the Pacific. Now retired, he has turned his hand to writing. His aviation background is reflected in many of these stories.

Set in Europe, North Africa, Hong Kong, New Zealand. Sydney, Honolulu, Christmas Island, Tahiti, Mo'orea, Rangiroa, and Bora Bora, it's a diverse and entertaining collection of fact and fiction, all based on the author's real-life experiences.

The dramatic engine failure described in *A Close Call In Tahiti* did occur, July 17th 1980, at Faa'a Airport in Papeete. The *Gun Running* happened back in 1957.

The author flew into Hong Kong's old Kai Tak airport many times. *Remember Kai Tak* describes just what it was like flying into that extraordinary place. The yacht, featured in *Andria,* is the *Jardilinka,* a well-known vessel in Hong Kong waters. The author was lucky enough to enjoy many cruises on this fine old vessel.

The Jury is a true story, as are, *A Curious Business, The Bottle,* and *Christmas Island. A Labs Attack* describes some of the things that went on during the Cold War, all true, these things happened.

Aerial topdressing features in *The Greening Of Northland,* an insight into this unique New Zealand industry.

I'm sure you'll enjoy reading these stories just as much as the author enjoyed writing them.

Flying The Pacific
(a memoir)

After several years in NATO's Second Tactical Air Force on the front line of the Cold War in Germany, the author returned to his native New Zealand and joined TEAL, Tasman Empire Airways. During a thirty year career with the airline he was part of the enormous expansion into the present day Air New Zealand. He flew everything from the jet prop Electra to the 747-400. The Pacific, the Orient, America, and during the later part of his career all the way to Europe. It was not a simple process however, there was a lot of angst and heartache.

This book is not just about flying, it includes everything else that's involved in an airline pilot's life, the travel, the 'holiday' stopovers, living abroad, interesting experiences, some of them very interesting, the stresses and pressures, the rewards, it's a rather unique lifestyle. Here's a sample of the first chapter.

Joining TEAL

'Got the checkerboard?'
'Yep, got it,' replies the co-pilot.
'Height ok?' I ask.
'Yep, looking good.'
'Ok when that tall building with the mast over on the right is
abeam we'll turn.'
'Yep it's coming up now.'

*'That wind's picked up, better turn a fraction earlier,' the co-
pilot offers.
'Yep, thanks.'
'Right; go now.'*

We are flying a DC8, it's Hong Kong's notorious checkerboard approach at the old Kai Tak airport. I bank the big jet steeply to the right and peer out looking for the runway, there it is, right on cue. It's a murky evening, there's a strong crosswind blowing us right into the checkerboard, it's bumpy, and we're in amongst the tall buildings. This approach is one of the more challenging things in aviation, not for the faint hearted. There's a stiff southerly requiring the use of runway 13, the south easterly one, and that necessitates the famous checkerboard approach, the one the passengers love, the one that takes you right in amongst the tall buildings. The downside is that when this approach is required there's always a stiff crosswind on the runway. We complete the turn onto finals, assess the crosswind, kick in some rudder, and prepare for the actual touchdown, still with quite a bit of drift on. Just before the wheels make contact I kick it straight; the touchdown is quite smooth. Hold the wing down, careful with the reverse, that wind is strong. We decelerate and turn off the runway. Another adrenaline fuelled Hong Kong arrival. How come I'm doing this? I'm 32 years of age and this is one of aviation's more difficult places to be flying, and in a big jet full of people. It's quite a story.

Cold War Warrior
(a memoir)

A true story about a young lad who grew up in Blenheim, New Zealand, during the 1940s and early 50s. He developed an insatiable passion for flying, travelled to England, and became a pilot in the Royal Air Force. He soon found himself involved in the United Kingdom's nuclear testing programme in the Pacific. This took him around the world and in just a few short years he found himself on the front line of the Cold War in Germany.

If things had turned ugly this young Kiwi, along with others, was going to unleash nuclear mayhem on Europe, and would no doubt have perished in the process. This is his story.

Early Days

'Ok Harry, here we go.' I nosed the big Canberra over and headed for the ground in a steep dive; at about 600 feet with the target firmly in the gun sight, I squeezed the trigger. Four 20mm Hispano cannons burst into life and sent a shudder through the aircraft, I could see the shells shredding the canvas target on the ground. When we were ridiculously close I stopped firing, pulled up hard, and climbed away. Harry, my navigator, was jammed up in the nose cone, he must have been terrified; again! We were at a live

firing range in the old West Germany practising air to ground gunnery, I was having a ball, Harry was not! How did I come to be doing this?

Well I was a front line jet jock in the Royal Air Force, actually I was in NATO's Second Tactical Air Force in Germany, how did I get to be there? it's a long story.

In our cottage, on a beach in Auckland, amongst all the wine glasses, there's a copper tankard, it's lined with silver and looks old and tarnished. There are some words engraved on it. *IN HAZY MEMORY OF SALISBURY SOUTHERN RHODESIA JUNE 1962.* On closer inspection the engraving's a bit rough, the Os look like Ds, however, the quality of the copper, and the silver lining, appears to be surprisingly good. This tankard is a constant reminder to me about the early part of my life, the part that now seems so very far away, when I was involved in the Cold War in Europe. On occasions I ask myself, did all that really happen?

Was that me thundering around Germany in a jet, right down on the deck, eyeballing the East Germans? Was it me out in the Libyan desert amongst the flies, the sand, the heat and the sweat, trying to toss a bomb onto a target from very low level? Did I really shoot up the Larnaca range out in Cyprus with those big 20mm cannons? Did I really fly around those Norwegian Fjords in all that murk, ice and snow? That gun running business in Tunisia, did that actually happen? Was that me flying over the vastness of East Africa, the endless deserts of the Sudan? Did I do that sabre-rattling for Queen and Country in Central Africa? Was I really involved in that nuclear testing in the Pacific in the 1950s? Did I really wander around East Berlin at the height of the Cold War? Yes I did, it was all part of my Big OE, let me explain.

Mercenary
(a novel)

Rex Macare, fresh out of the military, a highly qualified pilot; his apprenticeship's finished, now he wants the real money. His quest leads to the mysterious Mr Roberts who makes him an offer too good to refuse. He meets, and falls in love, with the beautiful Kate, a high end fashion model, and he soon finds himself immersed in a whole new world. A heady mix of big money, huge money, dangerous flying, high end fashion, and unbridled sex. It does not last.

The story is set around the world, the South Seas, Vietnam, Paris, Algeria, Australia, and the DDR, the German Democratic Republic, the old East Germany.

It's a fast moving story that I'm sure you will enjoy.

Mr Roberts

Bzzzz, I press the doorbell, 'Monsieur Robier?' no response, I knock, 'Monsieur Robier?' still no response, have I made a mistake. I'm sure it was two this afternoon, room 202. I push the door, it swings open and I recoil in horror. The place is a charnel house, blood everywhere. There's a body on the floor, throat slashed open, I feel faint, want to throw up, it's worse than a horror movie. I look closer, the body has been mutilated, clothing torn open, blood all over the place, it's Monsieur Robier. There's something on his chest, a note.

Rentrez chez vous Monsieur Rex, ne plaisante pas avec nous. Go home Mister Rex, don't mess with us.

French, English, my name, it's meant for me, shit! There's something else, his genitals have been torn off and stuffed into his mouth, the FLN's brutal calling card.

Albert McConachie's Bad Day

A three part tale about the slow decline of Albert McConachie's matrimonial life into total disaster. Albert, however, quite unexpectedly, finds love elsewhere. The three parts of this tale are interspersed with a collection of short stories that you will find entertaining and amusing. The trivial, amusing, and disastrous; childhood memories you can probably relate to.

Carrie Gray
(a novel)

A young girl leaves New Zealand for Europe, the big OE. She goes alone, wants to do her own thing, unrestricted by others, experience everything. A skilled boaty, she wants to crew on a superyacht; she disappears. Her boyfriend, Michael, becomes concerned at the sudden lack of communication and sets off to find her; he disappears.

Michael's father Frank, a retired detective, becomes alarmed and sets off to find them both. He discovers a frightening underworld of drug smuggling, murder, and prostitution, dominated by several powerful families. It's devoured these two youngsters from far off New Zealand.

A fast moving story of romance, adventure, and danger set in Paris, Athens, and Istanbul, and spills out into the Pacific.